RECREATION
and TOURISM

Sue Warn

D0752334

Series editor
Michael Witherick

First published in 1999 by:
Stanley Thornes (Publishers) Ltd

Reprinted in 2002 by:
Nelson Thornes Ltd
Delta Place
27 Bath Road
CHELTENHAM
GL53 7TH
United Kingdom

02 03 04 05 / 10 9 8 7 6 5 4 3

A catalogue record for this book is available from the British Library

ISBN 0 7487 4418 5

Designed by Giles Davies
Page layout and illustration by Hardlines Ltd, Charlbury, Oxfordshire
Cover design by Sterling Associates

Printed in Great Britain by Ashford Colour Press

Acknowledgements

The author owes special thanks to Bel: without her work, the manuscript would never have been finished.

In the writing of this book, the author made use of information from the following sources, to which she and the publishers acknowledge their indebtedness:

Fig.1.2 from N. Leiper, *Tourist Systems*, Dept of Management Systems, Occ. Paper 2, Massey University, Auckland, 1990; Fig.1.3 from B. Boniface and C. Cooper, *Geography of Travel and Tourism*, Heinemann, 1987, adapted from Cohen 1972; Fig.2.3 from 'Take only photos, leave only footprints', IIED Wildlife and Development Series No.10, October 1997; Fig.4.9 from *UK Travel Statistics*, Fig.6.5 from V. I. Smith, *Hosts and Guest: The Anthropology of Tourism*, 2nd edn, University of Pennsylvania Press, 1989; Fig.6.6 from G. Doxey, 'When enough is enough, the Natives are restless in Old Niagara', *Heritage Canada* 1976 Vol.2. no.2: 26-27; Fig.6.8 from D.W. Robinson in L. France, *Sustainable Tourism*, Earthscan: 178.

The author and publishers would like to thank *The Guardian* for permission to reproduce the extract in Figure 3.6, from an article published 1 September 1998.

Contents

1 Exploring recreation and tourism   **4**
A   Some basic definitions   4
B   The tourism system   5
C   Classification of tourism   7

2 Resources for recreation and tourism   **13**
A   Introduction   13
B   Climate   14
C   Physical conditions   15
D   Attractions   16
E   Access   18
F   Existing situation and other
    considerations   19

3 The nature of global tourism   **24**
A   The take-off in international tourism   24
B   Factors behind the tourism explosion   25
C   Patterns in the growth of global tourism   27
D   A volatile business   30

4 The changing British tourist industry   **33**
A   The catalysts of change   33
B   Phases in the development of British
    tourism   35
C   Rural tourism   37
D   Urban tourism   42
E   Theme-park tourism   46
F   The future of the seaside resort –
    the rock of British tourism   47

5 The environmental impacts of tourism   **50**
A   Introduction   50
B   Carrying capacity   51
C   The environmental impacts   53

6 The human impacts of tourism   **60**
A   The economic impacts   60
B   The socio-cultural impacts   64
C   The human rights issue   70

7 Can tourism become sustainable?   **72**
A   The new tourist   72
B   Ecotourism – myth or reality?   74
C   Antarctica – making ecotourism work   80

8 Looking to the 21st century   **84**
A   A 2020 vision   84
B   The role and responsibilities of
    government   85
C   The Galapagos Islands – a last chance?   89

Further reading and resources   **96**

Exploring recreation and tourism

Some basic definitions

The relationship between leisure, recreation and tourism is shown in **1.1**. They are three activities which are often grouped together because of their overlap and very obvious linkage. For example, GNVQ students can study 'Leisure and Tourism'; in higher education courses, students can major in 'Recreation and Leisure Management' or 'Travel and Tourism'.

Figure 1.1 The relationships between leisure, recreation and tourism

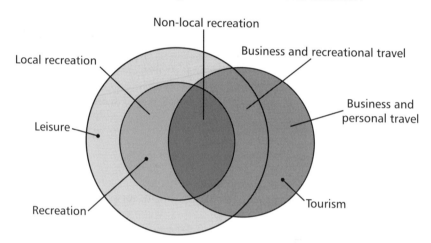

It is perhaps convenient to define **tourism** first, as this is the central focus of this book. Because it allows effective measurement of the volume of activity, a widely-used definition, both nationally and internationally, is:

> 'Tourism is all activity undertaken by people staying away from home for 24 hours (i.e. overnight), on holiday, visiting friends or relatives (VFR), at business or other conferences, or any other purpose, e.g. health other than semi-permanent employment.'

Tourism therefore includes non-local recreation, involving a stop-over, but technically it does not include any day-trip activity such as visits to national parks or cross-Channel shopping trips to France. **Recreation** is usually defined as any pursuit engaged upon during leisure time. There is an obvious overlap between tourism and recreation as they share many of the same facilities.

It is for this reason that the book is called *Recreation and Tourism*. It focuses on issues related to both tourism and day-tripper recreational activity. Recreation is itself a subset of the **leisure industry**, which includes 'all activities related to non-work time'. Tourism is by definition only partly for leisure purposes, as business activity can be a major component.

Review

1 In your own words, explain the difference between leisure, recreation and tourism.

2 To what economic sector does tourism belong?

SECTION B

The tourism system

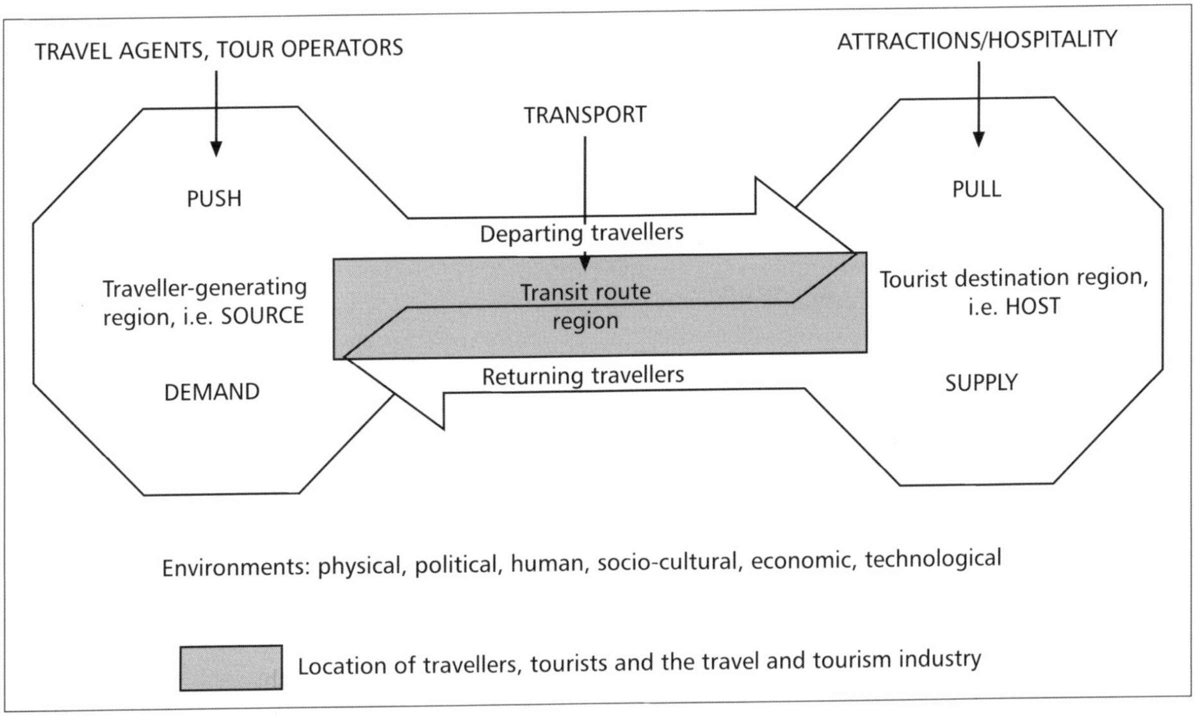

Figure 1.2 The basic tourism system

Figure **1.2** shows the basic tourism system, using a model developed by Leiper in 1990. There are three basic components in the model.

1 The tourists or travellers

Tourists are categorised statistically by the purpose of visit:

- Leisure and recreation – includes holiday, sports and cultural tourism and visiting friends and relatives.
- Other tourism purposes – includes study and health tourism.
- Business and professional – includes meetings, conferences, missions and incentive/business tourism.

There are many other ways of classifying tourists. These can range from cartoon stereotypes of life-style and behaviour to classifications based on the degree of institutionalisation and the ways it will affect tourists' perception of risk. Figure **1.3** shows Cohen's classification based on four major types of tourist.

		Familiarity
The organised mass tourist Low on adventurousness, he/she is anxious to maintain his/her 'environmental bubble' on the trip. Typically purchasing a ready-made package tour 'off the shelf', he/she is guided through the destination having little contact with local culture or people.	**Institutionalised tourism** Dealt with routinely by the tourism industry – tour operators, travel agents, hoteliers and transport operators.	
The individual mass tourist Similar to the above but more flexibility and scope for personal choice is built in. However, the tour is still organised by the tourism industry and the environmental bubble shields him/her from the real experience of the destination.		Environment
The explorer The trip is organised independently and is looking to get off the beaten track. However, comfortable accommodation and reliable transport are sought and, while the environmental bubble is abandoned on occasion, it is there to step into if things get tough.		
The drifter All connections with the tourism industry are spurned and the trip attempts to get as far from home and familiarity as possible. With no fixed itinerary, the drifter lives with local people, paying his/her way and immersing him/herself in the local culture.	**Non-institutionalised tourism** Individual travel, shunning contact with the tourism industry except where absolutely necessary.	Novelty

Figure 1.3 Cohen's classification of tourists

2 Geographical elements of tourism

These include (see **1.2**):

- The traveller-generating region which represents the market source for tourism. It provides the push to stimulate and develop tourism activity – that is, it creates the demand.
- The tourist destination is the reason for the tourism. The pull to visit destinations energises the whole tourism system to produce the supply of accommodation and attractions. At the destination, the full impact of tourism is felt. A key focus of this book is the evaluation of tourism development and management strategies.
- The transit route region is essentially the journey. It may be very significant, for example when Muslim pilgrims work their way across North Africa on their way to Mecca.

3 The tourism industry

Tourism is a truly global industry. In 1996 travellers took some 595 million trips abroad (77 per cent more than 10 years earlier). The World Tourist Organisation (WTO) predicts that by 2020 the numbers will have doubled. It also calculated that in 1996 the economic value of goods and services attributable to tourism was over 10 per cent of the gross global product. The tourism industry also sustains more than one in every ten jobs around the world, providing work for 255 million people. By 2020 an increase in the labour force of at least 100 per cent is predicted, involving an enormous range of jobs in tourism services.

Each of the three components of Leiper's tourism system (**1.2**) interacts with the others, not only 'to deliver the tourist product' but also to generate business in what is a truly global industry. Tourism is almost a unique industry in that the demand for it from the generating region is inherently volatile, seasonal and almost irrational in its cycles. Yet this demand has to be satisfied by destination regions where, unless properly co-ordinated and managed, the supply is often inflexible (in terms of facilities provided) and frequently fragmented.

Review

3 With reference to **1.3**, explain the difference between 'institutionalised' and 'non-institutionalised' tourism.

4 Describe the sort of holiday taken by an 'individual mass tourist'.

5 How might you explain the spectacular rise in global tourism?

6 With reference to **1.2**, suggest factors that will influence the strength of demand and supply in tourism.

Classification of tourism

Tourism can be classified in terms of the following features:

- **Distance** There is a fundamental difference between short-haul and long-haul tourism, and this has an impact on length of stay. A clear statistical distinction can be made between **international** and **domestic tourism**.
- **Location of the host region** For example, rural and urban tourism, or tourism at the coast and in inland mountain areas, leads to a markedly different development of activities and facilities.
- **Type of activity** For example, ski-tourism and health spa tourism are again distinct sectors, and many specialist activities such as birdwatching, scuba-diving and aviation all spawn more specialist niche tourism, sometimes in unusual locations.
- **Purpose** For example, business and recreation tourism are frequently complementary. Activities such as conferences and conventions have very different patterns and impacts compared with tourism for pleasure.

The most widely used classification of tourism identifies tourism by its style or approach.

Mass tourism may be described as a top-down, expert-led and planned tourism. As illustrated by the systematic development of the French Languedoc-Roussillon coast, it is usually very large-scale and designed for the package tourist market. The top-down approach is also often associated with the former planned economies of Eastern Europe. A good example was the constellation of planetary camping resorts on the Black Sea coast, such as Jupiter and Venus, designed for East German workers in the 1960s. They were all identical down to the design of the sequence of holes on the crazy-golf courses.

The capitalist model of mass tourism is dominated by market forces. It is typified by a tourism industry in which multinational companies shape developments according to world demand. Little regard is paid to the local communities, as in many Caribbean countries such as the Dominican Republic and Barbados. A current issue is the rise of 'all-inclusive' developments.

Figure 1.4 Major types of tourism and their variants

The rapid development of both these types of mass tourism causes considerable concern. They have an impact on fragile environments and cut across the indigenous cultures of traditional societies.

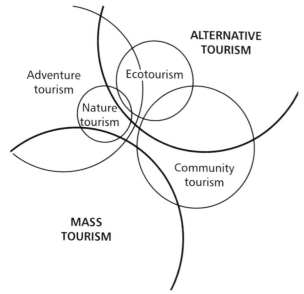

ALTERNATIVE TOURISM

Adventure tourism

Ecotourism

Nature tourism

Community tourism

MASS TOURISM

The Venn diagram in **1.4** suggests that there is no overlap between **mass tourism** and **alternative tourism**.

Alternative tourism assumes a bottom-up approach in that it involves local communities. It contrasts markedly with **mass tourism** in terms of:

- scale
- organisation
- type of tourist
- speed of development.

In alternative tourism, small numbers of individual travellers are catered for (as opposed to hordes of tourists), often by independent specialist operators or by local communities. One such example is the type of tourism marketed by the aboriginal community in Cape York, northern Australia. Development is small-scale, often using locally provided accommodation, and the slow, controlled growth allows the host areas to absorb the development.

While diagram **1.4** suggests a polarisation between the two sorts of tourism, in reality there is a continuum. Alternative tourism may contain some sustainable elements that make it ecologically bearable, as well as socially and ethnically equitable. But it also aims to be economically viable. It may grow into a more commercial form of tourism, as in the Khumbu region of Nepal (see **Chapter 6 Section B**).

Adventure tourism is usually resource-based and involves a physical challenge for participants. Whilst there are examples of small-scale and sustainable adventure tourism, such as nature hiking in Dominica (**Chapter 7 Section B**), some of the larger-scale adventure tourism, such as that found in the Victoria Falls area (**Chapter 6 Section A**) contains many of the features of mass tourism.

Nature or **wildlife tourism** is often seen as an off-shoot of adventure tourism but the focus is observation of landscape, flora and fauna. Where these natural resources are outstanding, many of the detrimental features of mass tourism begin to develop. Many national parks, such as Yosemite in California, or World Heritage sites such as the Galapagos, are victims of their own success. Finding future and sustainable ways to develop are a key issue (see **Chapters 7 and 8**).

Community tourism is tourism run by the community for the benefit of the community, such as the Campfire scheme in Zimbabwe or Farm and Cottage tourism in the townships of Donegal. However, as schemes expand, once again it is all too easy for mass tourism to take over and for the community to lose control. This happened with the community-developed Heritage Museums of Williamsburg in Virginia, USA.

Ecotourism is defined as 'tourism into protected natural areas, as a means of economic gain through natural resource preservation' (WWF). Although the participants have in common a commitment to environmentalism, they have very different ideas about the degree of comfort required. Many governments have leapt upon the bandwagon of 'green' tourism, but often there is more hype than reality or appropriate action. It is again very easy for ecotourism to grow so rapidly and be so successful that it starts to develop features of mass tourism, especially overcrowded sites. This is well shown in Costa Rica (**Chapter 7 Section B**). Tour operators in ecotourism focus on education, on landscape ecology and archaeology. Where they exist, local communities are involved in planning and operating the tourism. Many governments, such as those of Dominica and Costa Rica, take a concerned ecological view when planning tourism. The case study of Antarctica (**Chapter 7 Section C**) shows how control of access, price and legislation can lessen the chances of transformation into mass tourism.

Case study: A tale of two developments in Zanzibar (1998)

Background

Zanzibar's appeal is compelling to tourists. 'The Spice Island', located off the coast of East Africa, is exotic and romantic. It mixes African, Indian and Arabic cultures. Tourism came late and suddenly to Zanzibar. Since 1986 the government has actively promoted tourism for the much-needed revenue it provides. In 1997, 50 000 tourists visited the island.

Opinions are mixed about the benefits of tourism. It has created much-needed jobs, generated interest in local culture and provided money to protect historic buildings in Stonetown. However, there are major concerns. In a strongly Islamic country, 'clothes' (or the lack of them) are a major issue. Leaflets on dress and behaviour ('don't strip, don't snog and don't take photos of local people without their permission') have had little effect on the Italians, the main group of visitors. Italian hotels have bought up enormous stretches of coast for all-inclusive resorts. These use up scarce water supplies. The high prices the Italians pay go to the companies who own the hotels, while the local people are kept from the beaches by barbed wire.

Development 1 Wish you were not here

In an extraordinary transaction, the Zanzibari Government (supposedly with the blessing of local chiefs) has leased to an offshore development company for 50 years the whole of the north end of Zanzibar (Nungwi peninsula) for a charge of one US dollar. The area consists of 57 km^2 of land and is home to 25 000 people who live in 18 villages. The company has plans to build a £4 billion luxury resort area, containing 14 top-grade hotels, several hundred villas, a cruise-ship harbour, three championship golf courses and a new airport.

Many local people have not heard about the project. They have no experience of how to organise protests. There is evidence that public debate has been suppressed.

The impact of such a development is beyond belief – the sheer scale, the demands of a luxury foreign-owned complex developed in an area of water shortage. As only 8 per cent of the peninsula will be available for local farming, where will the local people go? The jobs offered are unlikely to be suitable for the local community who will lose their livelihoods as fishermen and subsistence farmers. Although electricity may be brought to the area, few local people will be able to afford it. Assuming that it could be financed, the scale of the project is just too big for an island the size of Zanzibar.

Development 2 Island of dreams

Chumbe Island Coral Park, on an island 12 km south-west of Stonetown, is the first protected marine area of Zanzibar.

Chumbe was discovered by a German sociologist Sibylle Riedmiller. It is one of the world's best shallow-water coral reefs. It has escaped the ravages of local fishermen because it borders the shipping channel into the port of Dar es Salaam; it has simply been off-limits.

Riedmiller embarked on a plan to conserve it. The only way to attract funding was to develop a tourist resort. So she developed a small eco-resort and educational project. This ran contrary to the government policy favouring high investment in large resorts. As Riedmiller said, 'It would have been so much easier if I wanted to clear-cut the forest and build a Hilton hotel'.

Review

7 'These two developments represent opposite ends of the spectrum of tourist development.' Discuss this statement by comparing and contrasting the two developments in the Zanzibar case study, in terms of their characteristics and likely impact.

Riedmiller entered the battle to conserve Chumbe with $600 000 of her own money and $330 000 from donations. The results are superb: seven heavenly state-of-the-art bungalows nestling in the forest, each built entirely of local materials. Each is equipped to catch, filter and solar-heat its own water. The toilets are of a composting type, so sewage is returned to the soil. A visitor centre has been built around the old lighthouse which serves as a viewing tower.

Five local fishermen have been trained to guide visitors through the forests and reefs, and also to keep out their old fishermen friends. The resort, opened in 1998, is a magnet for divers and scientists. It is also a resource for educating Zanzibari school children. It has won World Heritage status, UN Protected Area status and is to represent Tanzania at Expo 2000. All this, and it functions commercially as a tourist enterprise.

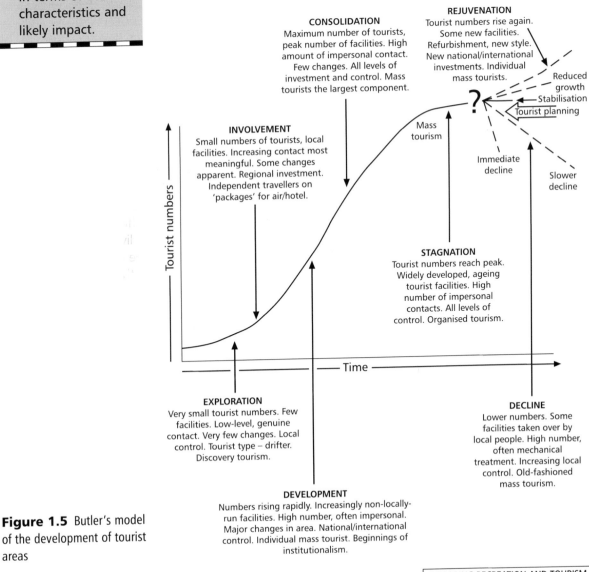

Figure 1.5 Butler's model of the development of tourist areas

So far in this section, it has been implied that the nature of tourism can change as an area develops. We take this point further by looking at a model devised by Butler (**1.5**, page 11). It shows what is known as the **tourist area life-cycle** (**TALC**). It is related to the **product life-cycle model** put forward by economists. Both models show how sales grow as the product evolves through the stages of launch, development, maturity and decline.

With Butler's model, the shape of the curve will vary according to the particular destination (**1.5**). More specifically, it will depend on factors such as ease of access, rate of development, market trends and tourism fashions, as well as the competitive strength of rival tourist areas. Planning and management at national, regional and local levels will also determine the way an area develops (see **Chapter 8**). Controlling the spread of mass tourism, and managing the destination after the stagnation phase, are other key matters. Benidorm and other Spanish resorts provide interesting examples of how destinations can rejuvenate themselves to avoid the boom-and-bust phenomenon, and can change direction and image in order to retain their tourist industry. Often higher quality can compensate for a decrease in the quantity of tourists. In **Chapter 4** you will have an opportunity to review the strategies for survival adopted by British seaside resorts.

Review

8 Draw up a table and write a one-sentence definition for each of the major types of tourism described in this chapter. Use this book and any further research materials such as those from Tourism Concern to note two examples of each. Write a short description to justify the choice of category.

9 Make a large drawing of the Butler model (**1.5**), then insert actual examples of areas currently at each of the seven stages. Select your examples either from within this book or from your own research.

Resources for recreation and tourism

Introduction

Like so many economic activities, tourism involves the exploitation of resources. The resource base of this particular industry is immensely diverse. There is likely to be some kind of potential for tourism almost anywhere in the world. But some locations appear to be uniquely favoured and as a consequence develop as tourist hotspots, whereas other equally well-endowed areas do not. In some cases, carefully planned artificial attractions can actually generate successful tourism in the most unlikely places. The 'Bradford – a surprising place' campaign of the 1980s was a triumph in the marketing of urban tourism in a location some would have regarded as unpromising. In the USA, every town fights for a share of the tourists with such seductive roadside signs as 'Cabbage capital of the world' to woo the passing trade off the freeways.

Figure 2.1 A classification of recreation resources

User-oriented	Intermediate	Resource-based
Based on whatever resources are available. Often man-made/ artificial developments (city parks, pools, zoos, etc.). Highly intensive developments close to users in large population centres. Focus of user pressure. Activities include golf, tennis, picnicking, walking, riding, etc. Often highly seasonal activities, closing in the off-peak season.	Best resources available within accessible distance to users. Access very important. More natural resources than user-oriented facilities, but experience a high degree of pressure and wear. Activities include camping, hiking, picnicking, swimming, hunting and fishing.	Outstanding resources. Primary focus is resource quality with low-intensity development and man-made facilities at a minimum. Often distant from users, the resource determines the activity (sightseeing, scientific and historic interest, hiking, mountain climbing, fishing and hunting).
e.g. Country parks	e.g. National parks	e.g. wilderness areas

Activity paramount ←————————————————→ Resource paramount
Artificial ←————————————————→ Natural
←———————— Intensity of development ————————→
←———————— Distance from user ————————→

Figure **2.1** classifies recreation resources under three headings on the basis of their quality and accessibility. It shows that in the case of recreational day-tripping, it is access rather than the quality of resources that counts. However, when it comes to tourism, the quality of resources may be of much greater importance.

Tourism is a vulnerable and highly volatile industry. The initial attractiveness of the tourism resource may decline, ruined by either internal or external adverse factors (see **Chapter 3**). For example, the impact of the Arab–Israeli wars left the highly sophisticated and well-organised tourist industry of Lebanon in ruins, and it is only slowly regenerating. Equally, tourist fashions are constantly changing and this prompts the frequent reappraisal of particular resources.

Pearce (1996) has identified seven broad categories of locational factors which have an impact on tourism development. The primary resources include the **climate** and other **physical conditions** such as scenery and landscape, as well as **attractions** like wildlife, history and heritage. **Access** has always been a key catalyst as it links the tourists to the area of attraction. Other economic factors include the nature of existing **land tenure** and **use** as well as the level of development of the host country. The last may influence the degree of government support. Secondary resources such as **existing facilities** are also very important. Many of these factors operate at a variety of scales, but **other considerations** are either more significant globally or influence the precise choice of local site.

Each of Pearce's categories is examined below in a little more detail.

Review

1 Explain what is meant by a resource.

2 Explain the significance of the variables shown by arrows in **2.1**.

SECTION B

Climate

Climate is a major factor in the promotion of nearly all types of tourism. The huge range of information, sometimes misleading, provided in the travel brochures is evidence of this. **Sunlust tourism**, as it is called by the travel trade, has led to the growth of an enormous range of tourist areas, from Winter Sun in the Gambia (the nearest destination to Europe with absolutely guaranteed winter sun) to Summer Sun in the Mediterranean. This is very much a 20th-century phenomenon, which may have reached its peak as a result of skin cancer scares. In the 19th century, bronzed skins were considered 'coarse'. The bulk of tourism then was winter tourism to the mild Riviera at Cannes and Nice.

Temperature may be significant. Resorts such as Darjeeling in the foothills of the Himalayas developed precisely because the Raj administrators wished to avoid the heat and humidity of coastal areas during the monsoon. Holidays in high heat areas are only possible for many people thanks to air conditioning.

Rainfall can also be very significant. In Britain, a wet summer can be death for domestic resort tourism, and all modern resorts such as Blackpool or Center Parcs (page 41) have to provide all-weather facilities.

Seasonality is a major problem for any tourist development. The aim of the planners has to be to increase tourism in the **shoulder period** (either side of the **peak**) and to try to find a new market for the **off-season**. In Florida,

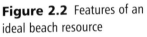

Review

3 Can you think of any other aspects of climate that are significant in tourism?

the British market has been vital to keeping the facilities going in the hot humid summer season. During that period, there is of course the additional 'excitement' of tropical storms and even hurricanes! Tourists are attracted to Florida by some of the cheapest long-haul prices in the world. Tourist locations in areas of extreme weather events, such as hurricanes, can expect significant disruption to their industry. The damage caused by Hurricane Georges (September 1998) completely 'knocked out' the tourism industry so vital to the economy of the Dominican Republic.

SECTION C

Physical conditions

Physical conditions, other than climate, are also very important both at a local scale and regionally. The nature of the site is very important for the precise location of a resort. Considerations include extent, geology, soil, relief, aspect and slope stability, as well as drainage and sewage disposal potential. In prospecting for new holiday destination sites, most resort development companies combine their site assessments with evaluations of other key aspects such as access and land availability.

Figure 2.2 Features of an ideal beach resource

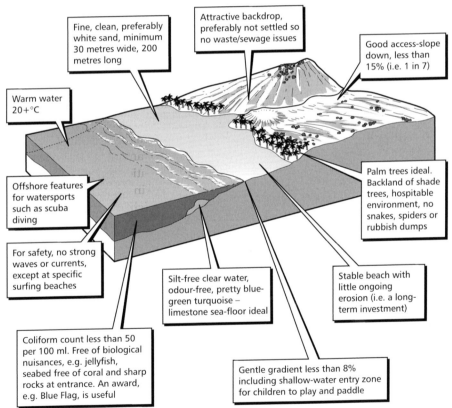

Fine, clean, preferably white sand, minimum 30 metres wide, 200 metres long

Attractive backdrop, preferably not settled so no waste/sewage issues

Good access-slope down, less than 15% (i.e. 1 in 7)

Warm water 20+°C

Palm trees ideal. Backland of shade trees, hospitable environment, no snakes, spiders or rubbish dumps

Offshore features for watersports such as scuba diving

For safety, no strong waves or currents, except at specific surfing beaches

Silt-free clear water, odour-free, pretty blue-green turquoise – limestone sea-floor ideal

Stable beach with little ongoing erosion (i.e. a long-term investment)

Coliform count less than 50 per 100 ml. Free of biological nuisances, e.g. jellyfish, seabed free of coral and sharp rocks at entrance. An award, e.g. Blue Flag, is useful

Gentle gradient less than 8% including shallow-water entry zone for children to play and paddle

Recreational resources such as landscape and ecology can play an enormous part in how successful a tourist development becomes. Figure **2.2** shows the features of an ideal coastal site. Many coastal authorities have to import sand for beach nourishment or to improve the colour of what is already there (golden sand is the aim). Others have to use groynes to trap sand, and this often causes a knock-on effect of sediment starvation down the coast. In some cases where there is pollution, the beach becomes incidental to the function of the resort. The swimming then takes place in the artificial environment of a fantasy leisure pool, as at Blackpool.

Natural landscape can also be a great asset, as for example an area of geysers (Iceland) or glaciers (Switzerland). Ideally, such landscape must have good access and quality facilities peripheral to it. Surveys have shown that most people rank forest areas as their ideal landscape for walking, driving and picnicking. This is especially so where they are combined with mountains. Forests have a high **psychological carrying capacity**, as groups are readily screened from each other. The fauna and flora may also provide a unique attraction, as in the Galapagos Islands (**Chapter 8 Section C**) or in the game parks of Africa. Figure **2.3** shows how decisions can be made to develop the most appropriate type of wildlife tourism.

Figure 2.3 Decision-making process for development of wildlife tourism initiatives

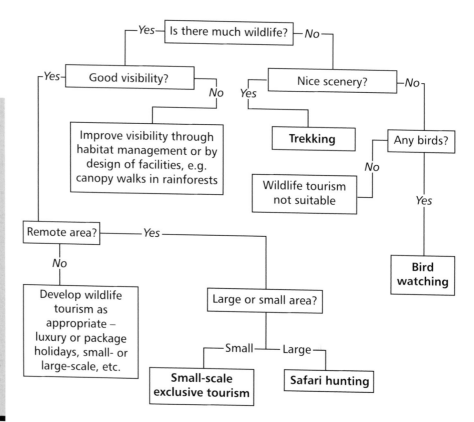

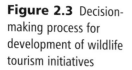

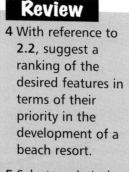

4 With reference to **2.2**, suggest a ranking of the desired features in terms of their priority in the development of a beach resort.

5 Select a relatively unspoilt area near you, and subject it to the decision-making process shown in **2.3**. What are your conclusions as to its potential for wildlife tourism?

SECTION D

Attractions

Successful tourism development involves managing the natural, historical and heritage resources to withstand the demands of actual and potential tourists. Areas with a high density and variety of natural attractions, conveniently located and accessible, will have a high degree of tourist potential. Environmental and historic attractions are considered so important that a series of Protected Area Management categories have been developed. These are sometimes supported by legislation to ensure their conservation for future generations. Occasionally, this is at the expense of local people's way of life. Figure **2.4** shows the range of categories. Many of the most difficult management problems are associated with world-class historical monuments. For example, there are the challenges of how to manage:

- the viewing of Stonehenge
- the monument erosion at the Acropolis in Athens
- the disintegration of the priceless cave paintings of Lascaux in southern France, where a replica set has been produced.

Figure 2.4 World Conservation Union (IUCN) categories of protected area

'Virtual tourism' may well have an increasing role to play here. Many more modern attractions such as battlefield tourism are more straightforward to manage.

Category	Type	Description
Ia	Strict nature reserve	Area of land or sea possessing some outstanding or representative ecosystems, species, geological or physiological features, available primarily for scientific research and/or environmental monitoring.
Ib	Wilderness area	Large area of unmodified or slightly modified land or sea, retaining its natural character and influence, without permanent or significant habitation, managed to preserve its natural condition.
II	National park	Natural area of land or sea designated to: (a) protect the ecological integrity of one or more ecosystems for present and future generations, (b) exclude exploitation or occupation inimical to the purposes of the designation and (c) provide a foundation for spiritual, educational, recreational and visitor opportunities, all of which must be environmentally and culturally compatible.
III	Natural monument	Area containing one or more natural/cultural features of outstanding value because of its inherent rarity, representative or aesthetic qualities or cultural significance.
IV	Habitat/species management area	Area of land or sea subject to active management intervention so as to ensure the maintenance of habitats and/or to meet the requirements of specific species.
V	Protected landscape/ seascape	Area of land/coast/sea where the interaction of people and nature over time has produced an area of distinct character with significant aesthetic, ecological and/or cultural value.
VI	Managed resource area	Area containing predominantly unmodified natural systems, managed to ensure long-term protection and maintenance of biological diversity, while providing at the same time a sustainable flow of natural products and services to meet community needs.
VII	World Heritage Site	Area of outstanding universal value, designated with the principal aim of fostering international co-operation in safeguarding these important areas through the World Heritage Convention.
VIII	Biosphere Reserve	Area designated to meet a range of objectives, including research monitoring and training, as well as conservation roles through UNESCO's Man and the Biosphere Programme. The human component of the programme is vital, and aims to establish a network of areas that is representative of the world's ecosystems.

Cultural attractions include living expressions of existing cultures such as dress, artefacts, religious rites and customs, dance and music. Attractions of this nature are very vulnerable to adaptation for perceived tourist taste, or contamination by mass tourism. This is well illustrated by the Masai dances staged for tourists on the Kenyan safari trail. Fortunately, cultural tourism is particularly attractive to explorer tourists and small groups involved in the cultural study type of tourism.

Developers can create artificial attractions, tailor-made for tourists. These facilities can fulfil the need for:

- **thrills and risk-taking** experiences, for example bungee jumping, white-knuckle rides in theme parks and gambling in casinos
- **entertainment, relaxation and social contact** by means of carnivals, festivals, restaurants and entertainment complexes
- **consumerism** – providing facilities to purchase luxury goods, for example via duty-free zones, factory outlets, antique fairs or leisure shopping at new complexes such as Trafford Centre
- **education** – providing galleries and museums; a major new museum can be an anchor attraction.

Well-designed resorts can more than compensate for indifferent natural resources. For example, Las Vegas was originally developed as a casino resort and for that reason was located out in the desert away from the law. It is now benefiting from being the 'fly' point for the Grand Canyon. It has moved on to become an all-round luxury leisure and entertainment resort with some of the most up-market fantasy hotels in the world.

Many modern developers work on the all-inclusive resort concept. Such resorts often require high levels of investment and can be very risky business ventures (witness the early problems with EuroDisney). They rely on a high threshold with all-year-round throughput in order to achieve economic viability. High-quality mega resorts not only generate tourist numbers but more importantly boost tourist spending. Inevitably, large complexes have a big impact on the local area. Some are designed to be multi-purpose so that they can be used by day-trippers and local residents too.

Review

6 With reference to 2.4, find actual examples of all the types of protected area.

Access

Access can be looked at in two ways: physical access and market access.

Physical access depends to a large degree on the existing infrastructure. This includes the location of access routes, highways, railways and the proximity of an airport, as these are very costly to provide. For example, when Sierra Leone ventured into long-haul tourism, largely from Germany and Britain, the air link was run by British Caledonian. Sierra Leone had no jets suitable for international flights. Before reaching the only two quality hotels at Cape Sierra, tourists had to contend with an extraordinary journey from the one airport. This involved a ferry crossing and a three-hour bus journey through Freetown. Isolation is only an advantage where 'hideaway' luxury tourism is planned, where remoteness emphasises exclusivity, as at Peter Island off the Virgin Islands in the Caribbean.

Accessibility is also measured in terms of proximity to the **market**, either in terms of travel time, cost or distance. For success at an international level, proximity to MEDCs (industrialised and urbanised countries) is of key importance. Even so, much of the boom in the long-haul market has been due to the annihilation of distance by the widespread availability of cheap jet flights.

Motorways or fast road access from urban areas explain why the Peak District National Park is so heavily visited. Market access is also vital for the second-home market in terms of nearness to the primary or main residence. A one-way journey of 200 km would seem to be the maximum range for the weekend market; hence the popularity of some villages in the southern Lake District with people from Lancashire towns.

Review

7 Identify and give examples of the different aspects of accessibility that are important in the development of tourism.

SECTION F

Existing situation and other considerations

Two of Pearce's categories (page 14) relate to the situation that prevailed before tourism develops, in terms of facilities, land tenure and use.

Facilities

For successful development of resort tourism, services and infrastructure are vital. For instance, in Belize, tourism has been constrained by a lack of reliable water supplies and efficient sewage disposal systems. It is frustrating because hotels, for example in San Pedro, could take many more people. One of the main reasons for the development of urban tourism was the need to promote weekend breaks at discount prices. This was to ensure a more even use of facilities such as hotels over the week, or to fill the gap in business tourism (for example, in Birmingham). Equally, conference tourism is a major earner in places such as Bournemouth out of season.

Land tenure and use

The purchase of land, or the acquisition of rights to occupy a site, is a necessary prerequisite for a tourism development project, especially for a large, planned resort. Planning permission is often very difficult to obtain, as for example for building second homes in rural areas. Such a development automatically raises the price of housing for local people, yet does not improve the viability of village services. Available land may be in short supply, particularly in small islands that are popular with tourists. It can become a real constraint. Some resorts are developed regardless of local people's wishes, as has been the case in Goa, India.

Many high-value areas, especially at the coast and in mountains, are state-owned. Communal land is often only made available for tourism provided the tribal chiefs are given shares in the development company. This has been common practice in Fiji. Private land may or may not be available for development; the main determinant of sale is frequently the price.

Other considerations

These include **political** considerations. Government policy for tourism has a major impact, with incentives available for selective regional development (as in Thailand) or for the development of urban tourism as part of an urban regeneration strategy (as in Manchester) or for rural areas (as in Pembrokeshire via farm diversification grants). Irish Tourist Development is a model followed by rural tourism as it spreads throughout the Irish countryside. **Labour costs** are often significant, especially in labour-intensive tourism such as cruise ships. At the same time, in order to get the quality of workforce, intensive training programmes need to be developed.

Review

8 Contrast the tourism labour recruitment situation in MEDCs with that in LEDCs.

Case study: Ski-field development

Ski-field location is heavily dependent on appropriate physical conditions, namely snow cover and slopes.

Snow cover is the main determinant of the length of season. Important aspects include:

- duration
- earliness of first snow
- length of snow-cover season
- quality of snow cover
- reliability of cover from year to year.

The last of these is perhaps the most important. Sierra Nevada in Spain was due to host the World Ski Championships in 1990 but no snow fell in time that year.

Slopes are important, as a range of slopes is needed to provide for a variety of skiers, from novices who need gentle slopes, to advanced skiers who need exhilarating runs. To build a resort there must be 2 ha of quite flat land per 400 ha of hilly terrain. Size of slope area is also important. The physical capacity of a ski resort is often linked to the number of tourists fed by the ski-lifts. Avalanche risk can limit the capacity of certain fields.

Climate conditions at the resort are also important, and not just in the context of snow cover. Wind is an important consideration because it affects the functioning of ski-lifts. Many Norwegian areas suffer from a high wind-chill factor. Temperatures also affect the quality of the snow, while sudden changes heighten avalanche risk. The attractions of the ski-field include natural features such as scenic cross-country ski trails and the provision of other relevant facilities. Aviemore in Scotland is the access point for the Cairngorms ski-field, but since the season is so short, a range of other leisure activities is provided. Range and quality of accommodation and infrastructure can also become an important part of the overall attraction (**2.5**). The value of a ski-site can be enhanced where it is linked by lifts to neighbouring ski-fields. Access to a local weekend market, as in New England, is also vital to the general economy of a ski area.

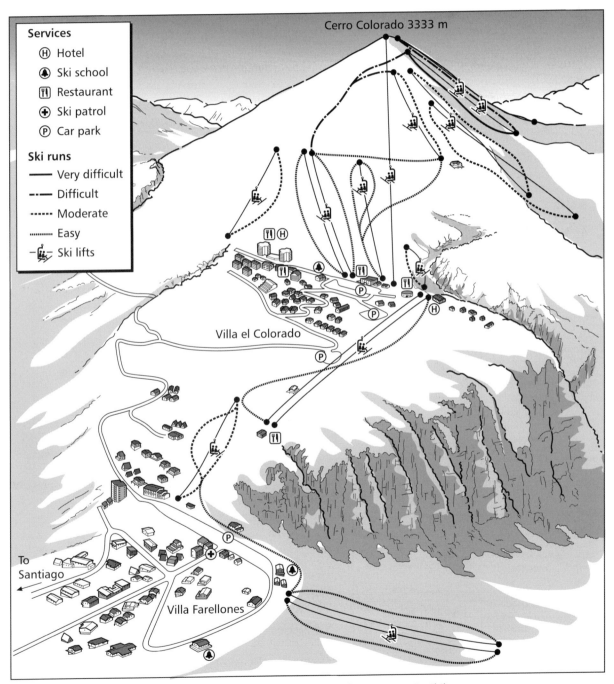

Services

- Ⓗ Hotel
- 🅐 Ski school
- 🍴 Restaurant
- ⊕ Ski patrol
- Ⓟ Car park

Ski runs

- —— Very difficult
- –·–·– Difficult
- ------ Moderate
- ·········· Easy
- Ski lifts

Cerro Colorado 3333 m

Villa el Colorado

To Santiago

Villa Farellones

Figure 2.5 Facilities at a new ski resort area in Chile

Figure 2.6 Factors favouring the development of new ski resorts in Chile

	Location/access	Facilities	Ski slopes	Altitude	Aspect
Portillo	152 km from Santiago. Road open with chains in a normal winter. Outstanding views	400 beds. International - class resort	12 lifts, 5281 m. All types of runs and slopes	2855 m, max. 3350	S
La Parva	60 km east of Santiago. Good views all round	Hotel. Apartments. Limited facilities	12 lifts, 9673 m. All types of run, good beginners' slopes	2816 m	S
Colorado/ Farellones	Twin resorts. 50 m east of Santiago on controlled-access road	Wide range of accommodation, 650 beds. Good range of facilities	16 lifts, 15 650 m. Excellent for beginners. Very extensive runs	2500-2700 m, max. 3333 m	SW
Valle Nevado	14 km access road, 65 km from Santiago. Opened 1998. State-of-the-art, still expanding	Chile's largest resort. Luxurious hotels. 800 beds. Apartments	8 lifts, 7000 m. More limited for beginners, excellent cross-country area	3025 m, max. 3670 m	S

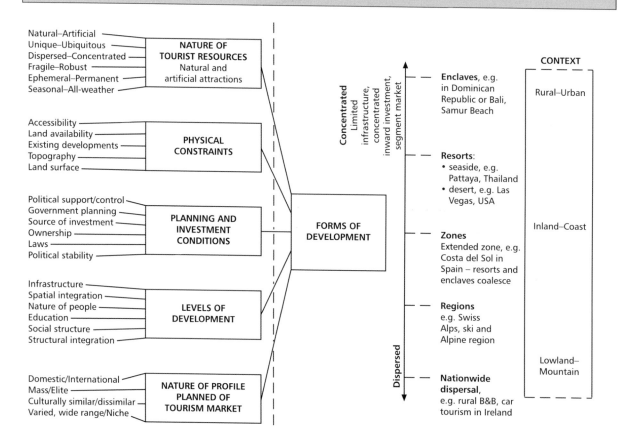

Figure 2.7 A student's guide to the tourism development process

1 Assess the relative importance of factors that determine the quality of snow cover at ski resorts.

2 Study **2.5** on page 21 which is a sketch of one of the recently-developed ski resorts in Chile. Examine and comment on the factors listed in **2.6** that have favoured its development.

3 Research a tourist development that contrasts with the area described in **2.5** and **2.6**, for example a resort in a long-haul LEDC destination. With reference to the development of your chosen example, assess the importance of the factors shown in **2.7**.
   a Draw the framework or use a tracing-paper overlay.
   b Insert the relevant details for your chosen tourist area.
   c Underline the type of tourism, and link it to the context.

The nature of global tourism

Two categories of tourism and tourist may be recognised: domestic and international (or foreign). With the former, the tourist's travel and spending are confined to their country of residence. The latter involves destinations abroad or overseas. The histories of both domestic and international tourism are long and closely interrelated. In this chapter, the focus is on international tourism and its growth since the middle of the 20th century.

The take-off in international tourism

To identify and interpret trends in global tourism you need to use statistics. However, the interpretation of tourist statistics is fraught with danger.

- Tourism statistics are frequently estimated, as they are often derived from sample surveys.
- Getting a representative sample of tourists is very difficult as there is such a diverse population to survey.
- The visits to friends and relatives (VFR) category is often informal and therefore underestimated.
- Not all countries use the same method of data collection, so it is very difficult to compare results or combine figures.

Figure 3.1 The growth of international tourism

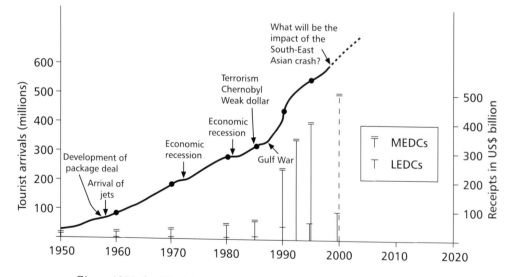

Since 1950 the World Tourist Organisation has been documenting international tourism. The figures show that the number of international tourists has increased by more than ten times (**3.1**). But the spectacular upward trend has been temporarily held back by a number of still-stands or 'blips'.

- The Oil Crisis of 1973 caused an economic recession that hit the tourism industry.
- In the early 1980s there was a world-wide economic recession. In general, people took shorter, cheaper holidays and domestic markets boomed.
- The year 1986 was one of disruption, caused by Chernobyl, renewed terrorist bombing activity, and a fall in the value of the US dollar. The result was a collapse in the North American market to Europe, as well as non-Arab tourism in the Middle East.
- In the late 1980s, the Gulf War obviously led to an almost complete cessation of travel to the Gulf and nearby areas such as Israel. Cancellations of luxury world-wide holidays increased largely because of uncertainty. For some mysterious reason, it even affected British bookings to Spain.
- During much of the 1990s the growth in tourism was linked to the emergence of the Asian Pacific region as a major source of international tourists. The crash of many of the Asian economies in 1998 will almost certainly lead to another 'blip', especially if it leads to world-wide recession. Conversely, the great Millennium extravaganza is expected to lead to massive tourist activity, not only in the South Pacific (a complex competition is developing), but also world-wide as people decide to do something special. It is also Olympics year, in Australia.

Review

1 Distinguish between domestic tourism and international tourism. In what ways are they closely interrelated?

2 Explain why the 1973 Oil Crisis hit the tourism industry.

SECTION B

Factors behind the tourism explosion

At least five different factors help to explain the explosion in international tourism.

General economic development

As countries become industrialised and urbanised, so standards of living rise, initially for the middle classes and later for the working class. The world-wide phenomenon of tourism therefore began in MEDCs in Europe and North America and later Japan. It then spread in the 1980s to NICs in the Pacific Rim and Latin America. Figure 3.2 shows how the pattern of the growth of tourism can be linked to economic development using the Rostow model as a framework. The gradual spread of paid holidays and increased **trickle-down** of wealth to more of the world's people have led to a related increase in leisure time and disposable income to pay for holidays. This is happening in Eastern Europe at the present time. Within the next 50 years, this may also lead to a tourism explosion in populous countries such as India and China. In MEDCs, early retirement and the ability of working people to take more holidays, or more expensive holidays, have also contributed to the creation of a genuinely global industry.

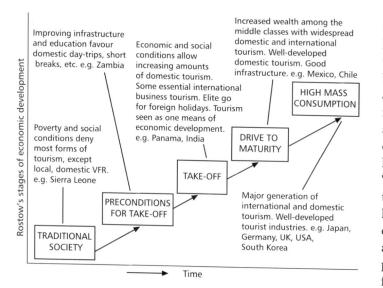

Figure 3.2 Economic development and tourism

Figure contents:

Rostow's stages of economic development (y-axis) / Time (x-axis)

- TRADITIONAL SOCIETY
- PRECONDITIONS FOR TAKE-OFF
- TAKE-OFF
- DRIVE TO MATURITY
- HIGH MASS CONSUMPTION

Poverty and social conditions deny most forms of tourism, except local, domestic VFR. e.g. Sierra Leone

Improving infrastructure and education favour domestic day-trips, short breaks, etc. e.g. Zambia

Economic and social conditions allow increasing amounts of domestic tourism. Some essential international business tourism. Elite go for foreign holidays. Tourism seen as one means of economic development. e.g. Panama, India

Increased wealth among the middle classes with widespread domestic and international tourism. Well-developed domestic tourism. Good infrastructure. e.g. Mexico, Chile

Major generation of international and domestic tourism. Well-developed tourist industries. e.g. Japan, Germany, UK, USA, South Korea

Changes in transport

Increasingly sophisticated, mechanised transport has revolutionised travel both between and within countries. Journey times have been dramatically reduced (the annihilation of distance) and long journeys have become more comfortable. The relative cost of travel has also become more competitive. The introduction of mass forms of transport such as wide-bodied jets, hotel cruise ships (flotels), cruiser coaches and high-speed train networks across Europe have all played their part in making global travel a reality for large numbers of people.

Changes in the organisation of the travel and tourism industry

The industry has come a long way since Thomas Cook's first package tour. The development of charter flights and package tours in the late 1960s was crucial as it led many Britons and Germans to take their first tour to Spain. Since then, new technology, such as fax machines and computer databases, has revolutionised the way holidays can be bought and sold. It is now possible to offer 'tailor-made holidays at package-deal prices' (to use a Kuoni slogan). Computers make all sorts of complex round-the-world transactions a routine procedure. Because of the high capital expenditure, they also encourage the formation of multinational organisations. Many of these, such as Airtours, are conglomerates in that they have business interests in airlines, hotels and travel agencies. They thrive by the mass-selling or **commodification** of holidays. The use of the Internet will also have an enormous impact on the travel industry. For example, it will probably lead to more opportunities for specialist providers to reach a larger market of individual tourists, by direct selling methods which bypass the travel agent (see **Chapter 8**).

Changes in society

The mass-media have increased general awareness of far-away places. Many people now have wider horizons and greater travel aspirations because they are better educated. They set aside a substantial sum for annual holidays in their budgeting. The consumer culture has encouraged people to seek out new destinations and try new experiences. The result of this has been the explosion of the long-haul market where people from MEDCs travel long distances both to other MEDCs and increasingly to LEDCs.

Changes in the global economy

As suggested previously, rising wealth is the driving force of global tourism. Changes in the global economy have ensured that the major tourist-exporting regions of North America and Europe have been joined by Asian Pacific and Middle Eastern countries. With the decline in communism, Eastern Europe and Russia are also becoming major sources of tourists. The one-time political constraints in those countries have been replaced by purely economic restraints. Many of the Russian tourists visiting areas such as Cyprus and Finland are wealthy and very big spenders; they represent the new capitalist elite.

SECTION C

Patterns in the growth of global tourism

Figure **3.3** shows that Europe is by far the most significant tourist destination region. It heads the rankings in terms of both money earned (receipts) and volume (number of international arrivals).

	% share of arrivals					% share of receipts				
	1950	1960	1970	1980	1990	1950	1960	1970	1980	1990
Europe	66.5	72.5	70.5	68.4	63.5	41.3	56.8	62.0	59.3	54.4
Americas	29.6	24.1	23.0	18.9	18.8	50.5	35.7	26.8	24.9	26.1
Asia Pacific	0.8	1.0	3.0	7.0	11.4	1.4	2.8	6.2	7.3	14.4
Africa	2.1	1.1	1.5	2.5	3.4	4.2	2.6	2.2	2.7	1.9
Middle East	0.8	1.0	1.4	2.4	2.2	2.3	1.6	2.2	4.3	2.4
South Asia	0.2	0.3	0.6	0.8	0.7	0.3	0.5	0.6	1.5	0.8

Figure 3.3 Regional shares of international tourism, 1950–90

Europe, like North America, is an area where large numbers of the population have a relatively high income (hence a high disposable income for spending on luxuries like holidays). Europeans have the highest average entitlement to annual leave in the world. They also regard travel as a spending priority. As many European countries are comparatively small, and there is enormous diversity of scenery and history, trans-European journeys are common. International travel is easy because of the excellent infrastructure. The growth of the EU also allows people to move freely between member states. Americans can travel long distances yet still stay in the USA and therefore not be registered as international tourists. Apart from the dramatic recent rise of the Asian Pacific region, the shares of the other regions like the Middle East and Africa have fluctuated because of wars or civil unrest. However, they remain at a lower level largely for economic reasons.

Rank		Country	International tourist arrivals (thousands)			Market share (%)	
1990	1996		1990	1996	% change	1990	1996
1	1	France	52 497	61 500	17.1	11.5	10.4
2	2	USA	39 363	44 791	13.8	8.6	7.6
3	3	Spain	34 085	41 295	21.2	7.4	7.0
4	4	Italy	26 679	35 500	33.1	5.8	6.0
12	5	China	10 484	26 055	148.5	2.3	4.4
7	6	UK	18 013	25 800	43.2	3.9	4.4
8	7	Mexico	17 176	21 723	26.5	3.7	3.7
5	8	Hungary	20 510	20 670	0.8	4.5	3.5
28	9	Poland	3 400	19 420	471.2	0.7	3.3
10	10	Canada	15 209	17 345	14.0	3.3	2.9
16	11	Czech Republic	7 278	17 205	136.4	1.6	2.9
6	12	Austria	19 011	16 641	– 12.5	4.2	2.8
9	13	Germany	17 045	15 070	– 11.6	3.7	2.6
19	14	Hong Kong	6 581	11 700	77.8	1.4	2.0
11	15	Switzerland	13 200	11 097	– 15.9	2.9	1.9
14	16	Portugal	8 020	9 900	23.4	1.8	1.7
13	17	Greece	8 873	9 725	9.6	1.9	1.6
–	18	Russian Federation	–	9 678		–	1.6
24	19	Turkey	4 799	7 935	174.3	1.1	1.3
15	20	Malaysia	7 446	7 742	4.0	1.6	1.3
		Total	329 669	430 801	30.7	71.9	72.8
		World	458 278	591 864	29.1	100.0	100.0

Figure 3.4 The world's top 20 tourism destinations, 1990–96

Figure **3.4** reveals a heavy geographical concentration of tourist arrivals. The ten leading destinations account for just over 50 per cent of the world's tourist flows. The last five years have seen a gradual diversification of tourist markets, with the emergence of new destinations, especially in the Asian Pacific region. Equally, in Eastern Europe destinations such as Poland and Czech Republic have all achieved sizeable gains in their world ranking. In spite of this, the top four destinations have remained remarkably static during the 1990s.

The situation changes somewhat if a table is made of the world's top tourism earners. Countries in the Asian Pacific region, such as Thailand, Singapore and South Korea, figure in this table largely because they are some the world's great shopping destinations. In contrast, a combination of low price levels and limited spending attractions explains why East European countries do not feature amongst the top earners.

The contribution to export earnings (tourism is seen as an invisible export and a great way to improve the trade balance) varies considerably from country to country. Jamaica derives 77 per cent of its export earnings from tourism, and is not even a top 20 destination, whereas Spain, the world's third most popular tourist destination, derives only 29 per cent. This reflects the fact that the Spanish economy is more broadly based than that of Jamaica.

Figure 3.5 The world's top 25 tourism spenders, 1985–95

Rank			Country	Expenditure (US$m)	% share
1985	1990	1995		1995	1995
2	2	1	Germany	50 675	14.2
1	1	2	USA	45 855	12.8
4	3	3	Japan	36 792	10.3
3	4	4	UK	24 737	6.9
5	6	5	France	16 328	4.6
10	5	6	Italy	12 419	3.5
8	8	7	Austria	11 687	3.3
–	–	8	Russian Federation	11 599	3.2
7	9	9	Netherlands	11 455	3.2
6	7	10	Canada	10 220	2.9
12	13	11	Belgium	9 215	2.6
17	14	12	Taiwan	8 457	2.4
9	11	13	Switzerland	7 636	2.1
25	19	14	South Korea	5 903	1.7
50	46	15	Poland	5 500	1.5
14	10	16	Sweden	5 422	1.5
24	22	17	Singapore	5 039	1.4
15	15	18	Australia	4 604	1.3
21	16	19	Spain	4 540	1.3
18	18	20	Denmark	4 280	1.2
19	23	21	Brazil	4 245	1.2
16	17	22	Norway	4 221	1.2
40	40	23	China	3 688	1.0
43	33	24	Thailand	3 372	0.9
11	12	25	Mexico	3 153	0.9

When it comes to generating or exporting international tourists, it is the MEDCs that lead the way. The Big Four (USA, Germany, Japan and the UK) dominate the market. The ability of a country to generate tourists depends on many factors. These include:

- The general level of disposable income and the disposition of its population to travel and to spend on tourism (**3.5**). For example, German wealth and wanderlust have made Germany the number one spender.
- The tourist attractions of neighbouring states. As distances and costs involved will be relatively small, the temptation to travel to those states will be strong.
- The nature of available air links, as for example the relatively cheap mass flight corridor across the Atlantic between North America and Europe.

4 Write an analysis of the data in **3.5** in terms of the level of development in the countries listed. Try to adopt a similar style to the section on destinations (**3.4**).

5 How do the lists in **3.4** and **3.5** compare?

- Organisational factors such as the freedom from restrictions and the competence of the travel industry in marketing and supplying attractive accommodation and good internal transport.
- Historic and cultural links can play a part. For example, the French are attracted to former French colonies or dependencies such as Réunion, Noumea or Tahiti, and this is reinforced by good connecting air services from Paris and other major French cities. Language and family ties are especially important to the British who flock to Australia, New Zealand and the USA.
- A variety of push factors can help swell the numbers travelling abroad, for example cold rainy weather, or a lack of snow for skiing. The latter is reflected in the two very distinctive winter flows of 'snow-birds' from Canada to southern USA and skiers to the Alps.

SECTION D

A volatile business

Figure **3.1** clearly shows that global tourism is susceptible to external influences, such as economic, social, technological and political changes. Murphy, a leading expert on tourism, has stated that 'the only constant in tourism is change'. Tourism is a highly competitive business to be in. It is often dependent on a wide range of factors over which the destination area has little or no control. Some are positive, but if you read the newspapers the majority would appear to be negative. These factors include:

- natural events such as extreme or freak weather conditions
- economic shifts such as changes in the exchange value of currencies
- political events such as the imposition of currency controls or the outbreak of civil unrest and war
- social conditions such as high rates of crime.

Tourism is also highly volatile because of changing fashions and tastes in recreational activity, locations and the sort of holiday chosen.

Whilst global tourism continues its upward swing, it is important to remember that this general trend conceals the fact that the fortunes of tourism in different parts of the world do fluctuate. This is another dimension to the industry's volatility. In **Chapter 1** we saw that many successful destinations experience cycles of boom and bust. The rank changes shown in **3.4** and **3.5** provide further evidence. Some of the business cycles, such as short-term seasonality, are very obvious; they are easy to detect but not to manage. Others which are much slower to build up require careful research and monitoring to detect. Business cycles within the global economy also have an impact. In times of recession, the first cuts in personal expenditure are frequently made with respect to holidays.

The survivors in this uncertain world will be those tourist areas which:

- develop flexible options to manage tourism and extend the local season

Review

6 Identify the factors that make tourism such a volatile industry.

- overcome negative medium-term changes (for example, shifts in holiday tastes or the ageing of an established clientele) and who maintain their long-term importance
- overcome the stagnation phase in Butler's model (**1.5**) by regeneration and by attracting a different tourist market.

Enquiry

1   On a blank world map, mark on the top 25 source regions of tourists (**3.5**). Insert the North–South dividing line. What pattern does your map show?

2   Use statistics (available from World Tourist Organisation) to produce three maps to show the pattern of tourist flows from **a** the USA **b** one European country and **c** Japan. Compare the three flow patterns.

3   Study the statistics in the table below and suggest reasons for the changes shown.

4   A number of factors determine the size and scope of the tourist industry within countries, and the flows between countries. Draw up a table using the list of factors shown below, and write a couple of sentences explaining the significance of each, with examples where relevant.

- Size of population
- Affluence of population
- Freedom from regulations
- Transport routes/access
- Historical and colonial relationships
- Price/currency fluctuations
- Climate

- Nature of cultural and environmental attractions
- Government policy regarding tourism
- Standard of living in host country
- Nature of political regime

5   Study **3.6** on page 32 which shows the life-cycle of tourism on Ibiza. In the 1980s such tourist areas were described as being in 'a vicious downward spiral no-one seemed able to break':

- **Tour operators** claim that the fault lies with the **Spanish government** which failed to improve the transport.
- The **administration** blames the **hoteliers** for low standards and indifferent services in low-quality hotels.
- The **hoteliers** blame the **tour operators** whose insistence on budget prices has forced them to employ fewer and cheaper staff.

a   Relate the development of Ibiza to the model shown in **1.5** on page 11.

b   Assess the likely impact of the three phases on the environment, economy and people of Ibiza.

Year	Developing countries		Developed countries	
	Tourist arrivals (millions)	Percentage share	Tourist arrivals (millions)	Percentage share
1980	53.2	18.7	231.6	81.3
1994	134.9	24.7	410.9	75.3

Figure 3.6 The three phases of tourism in Ibiza

① Island paradise

Undeveloped until the mid-1960's, the White Island was discovered by the Euro-chic and the rock aristocracy. Mick Jagger and the rest of the Lear Jet set basked in an exclusive sun while, elsewhere on the island, hippies set up camp and blew their minds.

② The package years

General Franco began forcible development of the island with concrete hotels and airports and it continued into the eighties. In 1986, 1.3 million tourists came into Ibiza and its neighbour Formentera, nearly half of whom were British. The once feudal village of San Antonio was soon filled up with chip shops and tattooed trippers. But the same influx brought with it UK club culture in skeletal form. In the summer of 1987, DJs Paul Oakenfold, Danny Rampling and Nicky Holloway found that loud music and no sleep went well with a drug called Ecstasy.

③ Club Mecca

Then came the all-night raves. Out went the lager louts, in came the teenagers from the suburbs. Holidays operators, already running a network of cheap self-catering accommodation, artfully established youth ghettos in resorts like San Antonio. The nineties have seen Ibiza become the mecca of serious clubbers. Between the end of June and mid-August, more than a million people – half of whom are still British – come in search of two weeks of unchallenged hedonism. Dance magazines such as Ministry now print Ibiza pull-outs as UK clubbers migrate for the season. Manumission and Cream are among the more prominent clubs there; a trip to the island now costs around £750 for a week.

The changing British tourist industry

This chapter looks at Britain, one of the five big players in global tourism. The aim is to provide a detailed case study of the impact of world-wide trends on one country. These trends include increasing international tourism and an increasingly diverse domestic tourism. They are examined against a background of an unremitting rise in overall activity.

In order to understand the structural, social and spatial development of tourism in Britain, it is necessary to take a historical perspective. The pattern of change in Britain has many parallels in other countries. In some countries, such as Japan, the time-scale is more compressed, while in others, such as the USA, the spatial trends are different because of the size of the country and the pattern of its historical development.

SECTION A

The catalysts of change

Four factors may be identified as the key catalysts of change.

The changing attitudes and motivations of people

Today, holidays are a normal feature of life, almost an entitlement for a year's hard work. In historic times, travel was difficult, uncomfortable and, in some cases, downright dangerous. In the Middle Ages travel was very restricted and largely motivated by health or religious reasons. It was only when travel became less arduous that people actually travelled for pleasure, as for example to spa resorts like Buxton and Bath.

Social and economic emancipation

Initially, this affected the middle classes and only much later the working classes. Most of the latter lived in the urban areas created by the Industrial Revolution. Gradually, factory workers were given blocks of time free from work. For instance, the textile towns of Lancashire all had a 'wakes week' when the mills were shut. By prudent saving during the year, sufficient reserves of money were often accumulated to pay for a holiday. Later, as a result of trade union pressure, workers became entitled to paid holiday leave. The Lancashire textile workers nearly all went to boarding or guest houses about a kilometre away from the seafront at Blackpool and Morecambe. Over time, a whole range of cheap alternative accommodation developed including holiday camps such as Pontins, holiday flats and chalets, as well as camping and caravan parks.

Advances in transport

Mass tourism has only become possible with the development of efficient and affordable transport. The railways were absolutely crucial in linking the urban masses to the seaside coastal resorts. Figure **4.1** shows how the seaside resorts nearly all had very strong links to particular nearby feeder areas. For example, Sheffielders went en masse to Skegness. More remote resorts, such as those in Cornwall, were often smaller and received their clientele from a much wider catchment area. Many seaside visitors came by coaches known as 'charabancs'.

In the second half of the 20th century, it was again transport that revolutionised holiday trends. The charter flight was a key factor in the emergence of packaged foreign holidays for the masses, while the impact of the motor car for personal travel was vital to the emergence of 'dispersed' tourism in rural areas.

Figure 4.1 Expansion of sea-bathing resorts in England and Wales, 1750–1900

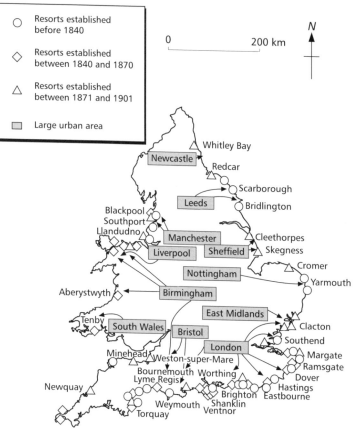

Organisation and infrastructure

The development of modern tourism has required the setting up of organisational systems, the provision of a supporting infrastructure and the training of personnel to run the mass tourism business. Accommodation, transport and entertainment were packaged so that all elements could be purchased in a single transaction. The British tourist industry was perhaps rather slow to develop domestic packages. But these are now very much part of the scene, especially the short breaks in urban and activity tourism and the 'all-in' holiday villages such as Center Parcs. Above all, efficient marketing is needed to bring the holidays to the consumer.

Review

1 Explain the significance of the railways in the growth of seaside resorts.

2 Define the term **package holiday**. Why have they become so popular?

Phases in the development of British tourism

As a result of these four factors, it is possible to identify a number of phases in the development of the British tourist industry (**4.2**). Each of them has contributed in some way to the extremely diverse provision and pattern of tourism in Britain today. There is no area that can afford to disregard tourism as a source of revenue and provider of jobs.

Figure 4.2 The changing British tourist industry

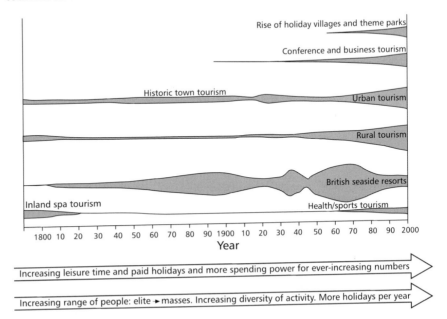

Phase 1 The rise of resort tourism (1800–1938)

In the 18th century, inland resorts were fashionable as a result of the practice of 'taking the waters'. This led to a tourist boom in the spa towns like Bath, Tunbridge Wells, Harrogate, Buxton and Droitwich. Although originally the resorts of the sick, spas gradually transformed into the resort of the fashionable elite who sought social pleasure at the theatre, dancing and walking. These spas were very elegant places.

It was not until the end of the 18th century that sea bathing was considered fun. The coastal resorts of Kent and Sussex, and above all Brighton, characterised this phase, with the rich moving their homes to the seaside for the long summer period.

The popular sea resort for mass tourism was not really established until the 1850s when the railways were built and a tourist structure was provided to meet a growing demand. Developments such as the Holiday Acts, improved pay, plus the establishment of Friendly Societies for people to save their money, all helped to encourage tourism. Figure **4.1** shows the general pattern of linkage between the urban source regions and the coastal destinations by the turn of the 19th century.

In the 20th century, the compulsory award of paid holidays (1938), cheap charabancs and the promotion of places like Skegness all helped to make the resorts even more popular.

Phase 2 Consolidation of the industry (1945–70)

In this period, three trends emerge: an overall growth in the market, the spread of tourism to new areas, and the beginning of the decline of traditional resorts (**4.3**). The last was a result of increasing foreign travel, but it also reflected the increased diversification of tourist opportunities, with people preferring to tour south-west England or Wales rather than stay at Blackpool or Scarborough.

Figure 4.3 The growth of British tourism, 1951–70

	No. of holidays (millions)	No. of holidays abroad (millions)
1951	26.5	1.5
1961	35.9	3.0
1970	40.2	8.0

Phase 3 Diversify or die (1970–)

This period has seen radical changes in the British tourist industry, not least in its organisation and co-ordination. The Development of Tourism Act (1970) sought to strengthen Britain's tourist industry in international markets by encouraging people to visit Britain, and by the improvement and provision of tourist amenities. These same facilities could also be used by domestic tourists and day-trippers, increasing numbers of whom now own cars.

This improvement in facilities has been spearheaded by the formation of a network of tourist boards, such as the Heart of England Tourist Board, to support and develop the industry regionally. The tourist boards promote and co-ordinate an enormous range of commercial, public and voluntary provision. A network of Tourist Information Centres (TICs) has also been established in order to connect demand with the supply, via displays, maps, brochures and a booking service. Central government also encourages initiatives and provides support for tourism through such schemes as the Farm Diversification grant. Increasingly funds have come from the National Lottery. Most local authorities now recognise the importance of tourism by maintaining a Tourism Promotion Unit as part of their economic development strategy. Many of these specialise in heritage and rural tourism (see Chester and Stoke case study, pages 44-46).

Figure 4.4 UK tourism in 1993

* Employed 1.6 million people in 200 000 enterprises, such as museums, hotels and restaurants.

* Earned more than £27 billion.

* Provided new jobs at a rate of 25 000 per year.

* Earned nearly £10 billion from foreign visitors, including foreign business people.

* Attracted 10 million foreign visitors.

* Provided 28 million domestic short breaks (1–3 nights) and 18 million longer breaks.

A number of different developmental strands can be identified which, since 1990, have made tourism the UK's most important single industry (**4.4**). Whilst London dominates the market, followed by the Bath–Stratford-on-Avon–Oxford triangle and Edinburgh, the statistics show an astonishing diversity of destination and activity. The following sections examine the strands that make up this diversity.

Review

3 Why did 18th-century tourists visit the spa towns?

4 Why did the traditional resorts begin to decline during Phase 2?

5 Suggest some examples of ways in which British resorts might diversify.

SECTION C

Rural tourism

In the 19th century, the Lake District, the Peak District and above all Scotland were always popular with upper-class tourists because of their landscape value. Gradually trips to the countryside developed, including charabanc mystery trips and organised group outings from clubs and factories. Many people became interested in cycling, camping and youth hostelling. The catalyst of an explosion in rural tourism included the post-war development of ten national parks in England and Wales, as well as rising car ownership (**4.2**).

In response to demand, a growing number of rural attractions such as country houses and gardens, wildlife parks, working farms, craft centres and rural museums were developed. These were listed in guidebooks and leaflets produced by regional tourist boards. The attractions could be easily reached by private car. New types of accommodation, such as country farmhouses, country inns, B&B and country cottages (often on farms) were made available to facilitate touring holidays. No part of Britain, even remote upland areas, was unreachable by car if there was a farm track. Sophisticated theme marketing also enhanced the coverage of Britain, with promotions such as 'Shakespeare Country' and 'Brontë Country' or packages linked to TV series such as 'Emmerdale' and 'All Creatures Great and Small'.

Whilst this rural tourism can have a symbiotic relationship with coastal resort tourism (i.e. they both feed off each other), the reality is that, in general, rural tourism prospers at the expense of resort tourism. Only a small number of seaside resorts are suitable as touring centres from which to explore the rural beauties of the national parks. Scarborough, Whitby and Tenby are three such examples.

The aims of rural tourism

The following six guiding principles are proposed for the development of rural tourism.

- The promotion of tourist enjoyment of the countryside should be primarily aimed at those activities which draw on the countryside itself, i.e. its beauty, culture, history and wildlife.
- Tourism development in the countryside should assist conservation by bringing new uses to historic buildings, supplementing the income of farmers and aiding reclamation of derelict land, as for example in former mining areas.
- The planning, design, siting and management of new tourist developments should be in keeping with the landscape, and wherever possible should strive to enhance it.
- Involvement in tourism should support the rural economy whilst encouraging a wider geographical and temporal spread so as to avoid honeypot problems of damage through over-use and congestion.
- Those who benefit from rural tourism should contribute to the conservation and enhancement of the countryside.
- The tourist industry itself should seek to develop the public's concern for the countryside, and understanding of environmental issues generally.

Whilst many tourist developments do fulfil the high demands of these six principles, a number of concerns have been expressed about the impacts of rural tourism. Problems associated with rural tourism are frequently exacerbated by the impact of recreational day-trippers who add to the pressures at honeypot sites. This is seen as a particular problem at bank holiday weekends or on sunny summer Sundays when both access and on-site facilities are overstretched.

National parks

The ten national parks, in particular, could be said to be 'victims of their own success', possibly because of conflicting aims:

- to conserve precious environments in the park
- to enable access and opportunity for a wide range of outdoor leisure pursuits
- to support jobs and the economy (especially farming in the park)
- to protect the local people's quality of life.

Enormous development pressures occur within the parks. Tourism is just one of these and conflict is almost inevitable. The quantity of visitors has now increased to 100 million per year and the nature of these visitors has changed from rucksacked walkers in the 1950s through car-bound picnickers in the 1980s to all-action sports people in the 1990s alongside a rapid growth of commercial ventures such as timeshare holiday centres (**4.5**).

Luxurious Lake District holidays on an exclusive private estate
45 JOBS IN £5M SCHEME

HOPES of 45 new jobs in the Lake District were raised this week with the announcement that a £5 million 20-acre development scheme in Great Langdale had been given the go-ahead by planners and residents.

The redevelopment proposal for the Langdale Estate includes 77 self-catering chalet units, a swimming pool, squash courts and extensions to the existing Pillar Hotel.

The scheme, the first of its kind in the national park, will provide 45 permanent jobs and 32 part-time jobs. There are at present about 70 caravans on site, used only in the season.

The new development, by its owners, the Langdale Partnership, will bring the site into year-round use, with the chalets being let on a time-share basis and with facilities such as the swimming pool being made available to local people.

Figure 4.5 The Great Langdale redevelopment scheme in the Lake District

Case study: National parks in England and Wales 'loved to death'

The Dower Report which led to the creation of national parks in England and Wales concluded that 'there can be few national plans which, at so modest a cost, offer so large a prospect of health-giving happiness for the people'.

Nearly 50 years on, the parks have become 'loved to death' and crowded to crisis point, with over 100 million visitors each year. They are threatened by cars and commercial leisure developments, such as new timeshare developments, as well as more intensive upland farming and creeping coniferisation. Some would argue that the British concept of national parks was fatally flawed in the first place. This was because it promoted both conservation of the environment and economic development within the parks, including mass recreational use.

In response to the conflict between these two opposing aims, numerous management strategies have been proposed such as omitting the top beauty spots from promotional leaflets.

The hardest-hit parks (those with greatest access by fast road from Britain's urban communities) have some extreme problems.

- In the Lake District, on one summer Sunday the police had to close the southern entrances to the Park because of a 10-mile traffic queue to get in.
- In the Peak District, visitor pressure has led to widespread footpath damage. The start of the Pennine Way footpath has become known as the 'Pennine motorway' because it has widened into an eight-lane walkway.

Fleets of off-road vehicles have wrecked 80 per cent of the ancient tracks on the moors.

Radical solutions to this problem of over-use include:

- imposing a visitor poll tax
- halving car park provision
- closing honeypot sites except to permit holders
- creating areas that can only be reached by park-and-ride electric buses
- spreading tourism to lesser known areas such as country parks.

In the 1997 Countryside Commission report 'Fit for the Future', even more all-embracing plans were proposed. The top priority would be the conservation of scenery and wildlife, and the recreational role would be down-graded except for appropriately quiet enjoyment. Recommendations in the report included:

- Allowing public access to all the open land of the parks by 2000; this would reduce pressure on existing public areas.
- Signposting and legally defining all of the 19 000 km of public rights of way in the parks.
- Ending military training over some 40 000 ha of the national parks. Some people would argue that these no-go areas, as in the Northumberland National Park, actually conserve ecosystems.
- Stricter control over traffic, with experimental car-free zones to encourage people to walk in to popular areas.
- Greater powers for the parks to direct tourism developments.
- Tighter planning controls, especially over mineral extraction.
- New systems of farm support to restore and extend wild areas by reducing overgrazing by sheep (a problem in the Peak District and Yorkshire Dales).
- An end to major coniferous forestry developments.

Such recommendations would inevitably require a tremendous amount of investment from public funding (estimated in 1991 at around £10 million a year); hence private sponsorship for certain improvements has been suggested.

As we move towards the Millennium, three new national parks have been created: the New Forest, the Norfolk Broads and the Cairngorms in Scotland. However, despite the adoption of some imaginative management schemes of individual areas, many of the problems identified in the 1990s remain the same or have become even worse.

Review

6 Study the five proposals put forward with the aim of reducing tourist over-use of the national parks. Suggest and justify a ranking of those recommendations according to their likely success in achieving the basic aim.

7 Explain how each of the eight recommendations contained in the 1997

Report would help ease the problems of the national parks

8 Study 4.5. Outline the advantages and disadvantages of such a scheme and explain why there was controversy about it taking place in a national park. Does it fulfil the six principles for the development of rural tourism set out on page 38?

There are two other controversial issues in rural tourism: the development of holiday villages, and the complex matter of second homes.

Holiday villages

These are large-scale developments and are best exemplified by the chain of Center Parcs villages. They are, in effect, inland resorts. Holiday villages have gained a firm foothold on the British mainland since their inception in the Netherlands in the late 1960s (4.2). They may be regarded as an example of **enclave tourism**; there is much concern about their impact on rural areas.

When they were first proposed, the English Tourist Board welcomed them, if only because they would generate much-needed employment. The first was built in Sherwood Forest in 1987 followed by others at Elveden (Suffolk) and Longleat Park (Wiltshire). Schemes tend to be in woodland areas with around 600 villas set in up to 200 ha of land with full village facilities, a sub-tropical leisure dome, restaurants and shops.

Overall, the villages generate around 800 jobs, but over half of these are domestic and two-thirds are part-time. Local purchasing by the holiday village is another possible direct benefit. Whilst local distribution depots are used for national products, a recent survey at Center Parcs Sherwood showed that under 20 per cent of supplies come from local sources. Indirect spending by visitors off site is another virtue put forward by developers, but the reality is that once the visitors get in, they very seldom escape! The only use of local services tends to occur during change-over days.

Surveys carried out among residents living close to holiday villages have shown the major concern to be the greatly increased volume of traffic on change-over days. Up to 3000 extra traffic movements have been recorded on such days. Other questions to emerge include:

- Why do the holiday villages not employ local retired people?
- Why are the jobs poorly paid?
- Why can't local people use the outstanding leisure facilities?

Although the actual economic benefits to local people are not as great as might be expected, there is no doubt that Center Parcs resorts are both popular and successful, especially for short-break holidays. They enjoy occupancy rates close to 100 per cent. The developments are also considered to be environmentally friendly. They are, however, yet another nail in the coffin of the seaside resorts.

Second homes

Second or holiday homes constitute a highly controversial issue. They are so common in some Peak District, Lake District and Welsh villages as to make them into ghost settlements during the week. A further issue in Wales is the Nationalist one: that Welsh homes are being bought by English strangers and that Welsh people are priced out of housing that is only used for part of the year. So strong has been the resentment that in the 1980s Welsh Nationalist supporters undertook arson attacks on English second homes. Other aspects of the second home issue are illustrated in **4.6**.

Figure 4.6 Weekend visitors arriving at their second homes in a quiet country village

Review

9 Draw up a table to show the pros and cons of holiday villages in terms of their impact on the environment and local community.

10 Look at **4.6** which highlights some of the issues posed by the increasing number of second homes in many rural villages. Write an assessment of the advantages and disadvantages of the second home and holiday cottage industry.

SECTION D

Urban tourism

Historic and cathedral cities such as York, Chester and Bath, and the capital cities of London, Edinburgh and Cardiff with their galleries, museums and theatres, have for a long time been powerful magnets to tourists (**cultural tourism**). But Britain's industrial towns were seen as 'places to escape from'. In the 1970s, however, a new type of urban tourism began to emerge (**4.2**). It was particularly associated with short breaks and day-trips, and it encompassed leisure shopping in factory outlets and mega-malls such as the MetroCentre at Gateshead, as well as cultural and heritage tourism.

Heritage tourism is difficult to classify, as it includes old industrial sites. Some of these are found in rural areas (it might be an old water mill) but the majority are found in industrial urban areas. Features such as restored canals, old docks and warehouses have become centres of tourist interest. The development of this new heritage tourism is now a key factor in the urban regeneration schemes of cities like Liverpool, Leeds, Bradford and Manchester, and again contributes to the spatial spread of tourism across Britain. Whereas towns such as Canterbury or Oxford always had a tourism strategy, they are now joined by towns such as Stoke-on-Trent, Wigan and Dudley, all members of a new generation of up-and-coming tourist towns. All sorts of reasons are cited for the rise of heritage tourism, including nostalgia for the past, a reinvention of Britishness, and de-industrialisation. The last has certainly created a valuable legacy of redundant sites and buildings to restore. The breadth of heritage tourism is astonishing, and it appeals to a tremendously wide range of people. In an ageing society, there are now many people who are interested in looking back to their childhood.

Success in attracting tourists to urban destinations is strongly linked to **cultural tourism,** a current growth section in the global market. Whilst tourist products have always been developed in and around historic cities, the use of contemporary cultural resources and heritage is very much a product of the late 20th century. The conservation of cultural resources and the transformation of them into tourist products can be a real incentive to reviving traditional cultural identity, for example Yorkshire customs and food. At the same time, cultural tourism provides an opportunity to celebrate contemporary multi-ethnic culture. The highly successful gastronomic 'curry trail' marketed as 'Tastes of India' in Bradford is one such example. Actions such as these create a good climate for the investment and development that are crucial to the overall process of urban regeneration.

Historic cities such as Canterbury and Bath have a limited carrying capacity and have taken steps to manage the stress to the community and the environment caused by tourism overload. Some of the newcomers to tourism, such as Manchester and Sheffield, can take large numbers of tourists, especially where there are diverse and spatially dispersed attractions.

The new urban tourism is encouraged by the fact that, since the 1970s, the cities concerned have been losing economic activities because of decentralisation. They have badly needed replacement activities to generate income and new jobs. A highly successful example of such a scheme is the Albert Dock in Liverpool, funded by the Mersey Urban Development Corporation. The decline of the CBD fringe and inner-city areas left behind many hectares of derelict land. These **brownfield sites** represent an opportunity for physical regeneration and for the provision of leisure facilities for local people. Festival Park (Stoke-on-Trent) contains a multiplex cinema, waterworld, 10-pin bowling and a dry ski slope, and was created in 1986 on the site of a derelict steelworks.

Renewal of inner districts can also reverse the out-migration of residents, and attract back some of the middle classes who were lost by filtering to the leafy outer suburbs. It is also apparent that many facilities such as hotels and transport are fully used during the week (80 per cent occupancy rates) for business purposes, but remain relatively empty at the weekend – so urban tourism weekend breaks make economic sense. Establishing some types of urban tourism such as conference tourism does, however, require major investment, as with the new conference centre and hall at Birmingham.

It is also wise for any town or city wishing to develop urban tourism to assess its possible attractions. Bradford, which developed as a market leader with its 'Bradford – the surprising place' campaign, already had the attraction of proximity to the Brontë country. But it also refurbished the Alhambra (one of Britain's best-preserved Edwardian theatres) and in 1983 established the National Museum of Photography, Film and Television in joint partnership with the Science Museum in London, as artificial 'anchor' attractions. In 1996 tourism in Bradford was worth £64 million with a total of over 5 million visitor attendances at the top 12 attractions. Not surprisingly, urban planners have thought 'why not our city or town too?'.

Nearly all the Millennium grants associated with tourism have been used to create artificial attractions, such as the Millennium Dome at Greenwich (London). Undoubtedly they will draw in large numbers of tourists and day-trippers to towns and cities, thus reinforcing the further development of urban tourism.

Case study: A tale of two cities – Chester and Stoke-on-Trent

Chester

Chester is a classic historic town, with a cathedral, walls and a well-preserved medieval core containing many outstanding buildings. For this reason, it is on the 'national tourist circuit' and ranks with places such as York and Bath as a magnet to overseas visitors (**4.7**). Success as a tourist honeypot, however, brings with it the problem of congestion, both spatially within the town and seasonally. There is an extremely high visitor-to-host ratio, and while tourism does secure numerous jobs, many residents feel overwhelmed by the high profile of tourism in the city centre. Feelings of xenophobia can develop.

An extract from a tourist's diary gives the 'feel' of Chester today:

'Like many people in the hotel, I decided to take a two-day break in Chester to see the sights. The first mistake I made was to drive in. It was extremely congested and it took a long time to find a parking space. Chester itself was really interesting, with a very useful tourist office. I found I could walk to all the main museums and the cathedral. However, it did feel extremely crowded; in some of the narrow streets you had to fight your way through. The shops were wonderful, but I did have a concern about some of the shop signs, as they didn't always fit in with the black and white Tudor buildings. The place seemed to be full of streams of foreign school children all on day visits.'

Figure 4.7 Tourism profiles, 1996

	Chester	Stoke-on-Trent
Visitor numbers:	2.2 million	2.6 million
Overseas visitors:	34%	20%
Staying overnight:	39%	14%
Main activity:	Sightseeing (70%)	Factory shopping (51%)
Access by car:	63%	78%
Total visitor spending:	£110 million	£119 million
No. employed in tourism:	5000+	6600

Stoke-on-Trent

The growth of Stoke-on-Trent as a tourist centre only began about 15 years ago. The key catalyst was the 1986 Garden Festival, held on a large derelict site, and the subsequent development of a leisure, retail and hotel complex now known as Festival Park. This really helped to put Stoke-on-Trent on the 'visitor map'. Before this, people just passed by the city on the M6 and considered it to be a dirty, smoky, industrial place. In 1986 the city developed a Promotion and Tourism Unit. By 1996 the profile of Stoke-on-Trent as a tourist destination had grown significantly (**4.7**). The city now attracts large numbers of visitors who come specifically to see the ceramics (pottery and porcelain) museums, such as the one at Wedgwood, and to enjoy shopping, especially at the factory outlets. Increasingly the ceramics industry is seen as a unique heritage feature. There is also the possibility of Stoke becoming a short-break centre for exploring the Staffordshire countryside. Tourism is now a more important source of employment in the city than the pottery industry.

An extract from a tourist's diary gives the 'feel' of Stoke-on-Trent today:

'Like a lot of people I came for a "smash and grab" raid on the factory shops. We needed some new dinner plates and you can get quality "seconds" at about a third of the price. I came by car for the day and went round about five factory shops. I actually spent over £100 as there were so many bargains. My trip took about six hours largely because Stoke-on-Trent is such a confusing place. There were six individual towns which are all joined together, so navigation was a real problem.

11 Draw a simple Venn diagram which defines the nature of **heritage**, **historic**, **rural**, **cultural** and **urban tourism**. Are they competing for the same markets?

12 Analyse the contrasting profiles in **4.7** and suggest reasons for their differences.

13 Assume the role of a tourist officer and devise a five-point tourist action plan for the future development of tourism in Chester and Stoke-on-Trent.

The people were really friendly and always helped me find the way. Stoke-on-Trent looked a lot nicer than I remembered it, as many of the derelict sites have been redeveloped. I wondered about coming for a weekend break next time as there seemed to be a modern shopping centre, one or two interesting museums as well as a lively stretch of canal with bottle kilns. I came in from the North and I don't remember seeing any quality hotels, so I'll have to check on this before I return.'

Urban tourism is now a well-established and growing market (**4.2**). Most large cities have recognised the significance of tourism and have strategies for its continued development. Many historic towns are victims of their own success, with mass tourism now having the potential to destroy the very things visitors come to see. Whilst clustered attractions are convenient for visitors, spatially spread attractions as at the Iron Bridge World Heritage Site, are potentially easier to manage once a scheme for visitor transport between sites has been developed. There are always new ideas coming along, as for example:

- if a large 19th-century factory closes
- if a niche for a new museum emerges
- if a TV series or film focuses on a particular area (e.g. 'Full Monty' trail in Sheffield).

Much of the new urban tourism draws on a regional catchment and interestingly generates repeat visits. So if tourism units get the product right, and market new experiences effectively, there is no reason why jobs in tourism should not become secure and prestigious. Urban tourism does compete with weekend breaks at seaside resorts.

SECTION E

Theme-park tourism

Another development in the last 20 years has been in theme parks or **themed tourism** (**4.2**). A **theme park** can be defined as 'a self-contained family entertainment complex, designed to reflect a common theme'. The theme might be a hall of fame for a baseball or football team, it could be imaginary such as a magic kingdom, or it could be a type of experience such as the Wild West. The theme can be represented via landscapes, rides, performance and exhibitions. Many theme parks are filled with 'white knuckle' adventure rides. They owe their origins to North American fairgrounds in the 1920s and initially were largely a North American development promoted by Disney. There were also parallels in some European countries such as Tivoli Gardens (Denmark) and Effeling Park (Netherlands). The theme park concept is now globalised. Theme parks are extremely popular across Europe and around the Pacific Rim as well as in North America. The Japanese adore them!

Figure 4.8 The top ten crowd-pullers in the UK (1998)

Number of visitors (millions)	
Alton Towers	2.80
Chessington	1.75
Frontierland	1.30
Legoland	1.28
Flamingoland	1.15
Drayton Manor Park	1.05
Thorpe Park	0.97
American Adventure	0.60
Flambards	0.50
Camelot	0.47

In Britain theme parks represent the ultimate family fun-day out. Around 13 million people visited Britain's top 15 parks last year (and this is increasing steadily) and by the year 2000 spending on theme parks is expected to top £250 million. At present, most British theme parks are out of doors and therefore only open from March to November. However, the latest plans for theme parks such as the Millennium Dome are for all-weather, year-round provision. Because of the sheer volume of visitors to the major theme parks (**4.8**), their impact on the local area is a major issue. The top attraction, Alton Towers, has only just built an on-site hotel to encourage two-day visits and has to be reached via the back roads of rural Staffordshire. Access by coach is therefore another pressing issue.

The increasing trend is for theme parks to be owned by multinational leisure companies. This is encouraged by the high capital cost of development and also the high costs of keeping up to date with the technology to produce 'the necessary rush of adrenalin' gained from the biggest and best roller-coaster. The 21st century will almost certainly welcome new and larger theme parks, as for example on the high-quality environment of Rainham Marshes in Essex.

The future of the seaside resort – the rock of British tourism

Theme parks, like all the other diverse new developments in British tourism, challenge the future of the traditional British seaside resort.

In particular, they attract day-trippers and are in direct competition with the 'roller-coasters of the funfairs of Blackpool'. Moreover, they attract many of the higher-spending tourists who are vital to the survival of the seaside resort.

The seaside resorts are under pressure from all sides, and not just from tourism within Britain (**4.9**).

■ More British people are taking their main holidays abroad.

Figure 4.9 Holiday-making trends in the UK

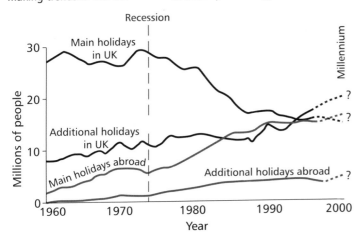

- If they do take their main holiday in the UK, British people are increasingly enjoying different kinds of holidays, such as car touring in scenic areas like the West Country, Scotland and Wales.
- British people now have a huge variety of short-break tourist provision, such as rural cottage holidays, urban heritage and theme park visits.

This reshaping of the geography of British tourism has posed a major challenge to the great British seaside resort (**4.10**). It emphasises the stark alternatives posed by Butler's TALC model (**1.5**): die slowly; stagnate; grow at a reduced rate perhaps in a new direction, or regenerate and rejuvenate.

Figure 4.10 A model of the traditional seaside resort in decline

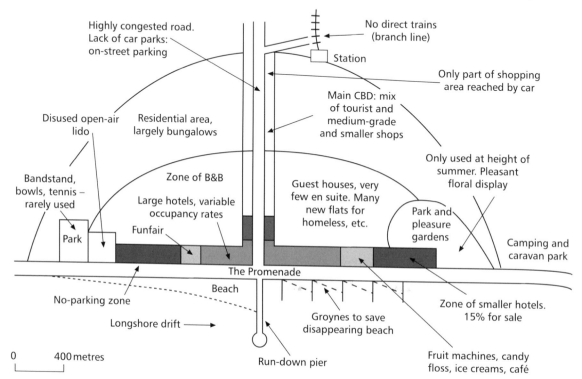

Reasons for decline of the seaside resort can be summarised as follows:

- the loss of traditional markets for holidays (down 30 per cent from 1965)
- the decline in long stays at the expense of day-trippers and weekenders has led to the closure of many small hotels or a change of use
- the ageing and down-market movement of the tourist clientele – nearly three-quarters of today's visitors to traditional seaside resorts are believed to be working-class
- low spending patterns mean a loss of income which in turn leads to reduced investment, diminished attraction and a loss of image
- many facilities are in decline and there are above-average levels of poverty and unemployment.

Clearly, decisions need to be made about the future of the seaside resort. Strategies for survival include:

- attracting development grants for refurbishment (e.g. when a private company takes over and improves a large hotel) or redevelopment (for building new shopping malls, leisure centres, conference facilities and marinas, etc.)
- developing short breaks with spring, winter, and autumn attractions (lights, festivals, targeted bargain breaks for pensioners and students) to ensure a more even flow of business throughout the year
- providing for business and conference tourism
- moving into 'pseudo' resort functions, for example converting guest houses and small hotels into retirement homes and flats or, more controversially, taking on homeless contracts with the DHSS
- accepting that the beach, deckchairs and open-air facilities must be replaced by upgraded leisure domes like Blackpool's Sandcastle
- refurbishing existing entertainment facilities so as to compete with large cities and theme parks
- improving the range of self-catering opportunities to cut rising costs; this would include providing extensive caravan and camping sites
- upgrading existing shopping facilities, eating places and public parks
- establishing a distinctive market identity
- improving car access by providing adequate and cheap car parking, and segregating pedestrian traffic
- upgrading the top hotels to 4- or 5-star ratings.

The basic aim should be to achieve a 'critical mass' for survival that is focused on year-round business. Both the tourist quantity and quality are vital if revenues are to be increased.

Enquiry

1 Select a British seaside resort and find out what steps have been taken to ensure the resort's continuing prosperity.

2 Collect information about one of Britain's major theme parks that will allow you to make an assessment of its impact on the local area.

3 Read through this chapter again.
   a Write a detailed analysis and explanation of the holiday-making trends shown in **4.2**.
   b Make a copy of **4.10** and annotate your diagram to explain the changing tourist patterns shown.

4 Study **4.9** and research the present state of tourism in a British coastal resort. Draw an annotated diagram to show your own plans for its survival. Use **4.10** as a base map.

5 With reference to detailed examples, discuss the factors that have led to the changing nature of the British tourist industry. Refer to a selection of the textbooks recommended at the end of the book in preparing your essay.

The environmental impacts of tourism

Introduction

The impact of tourism on any destination is determined by a number of factors. Of these, the following are of particular significance:

- The fragility and vulnerability of the local environment including its landscape, flora and fauna.
- The size of the destination area.
- The scale and rate of tourist development.
- The type of tourism – is it spatially concentrated, high-intensity tourism or is it low-density and dispersed?
- The level of economic development of the area. This may determine the degree of foreign ownership and how much economic benefit the host area derives from tourism.
- The structure of the host economy, especially the wealth gap within it.
- The size of the gap, in socio-cultural terms, between the hosts and the tourists.
- The nature and degree to which the host community is involved in tourism and their attitude towards it.
- The degree and effectiveness of any planning undertaken by the government and others to provide attractive facilities and an efficient infrastructure.

The impacts are usually considered in terms of **environmental** (often seen as negative), **economic** (perceived as beneficial) and **socio-cultural** (again frequently perceived as negative). It is the overall assessment of costs versus benefits that should be undertaken in each destination.

Clearly tourism can have very positive impacts, but regrettably – especially with mass tourism – it is the **negative externalities** that are so well documented. Successful management of tourism can limit the magnitude of the negative impacts and sway the balance towards an overall positive effect.

Review

1 Explain the significance of each of the bullet points above as a factor affecting the impact of tourism.

2 Check that you understand the meaning of **negative externalities**.

Carrying capacity

An understanding of the concept of **carrying capacity** is vital. This can be defined individually for each destination as 'the level of tourist activity which can be sustained in the long term without creating serious or irreversible changes to the people's lives and environment'. If the carrying capacity is exceeded, then the destination will be dominated by rapidly increasing negative effects, and any positive strengths will be lost.

Optimum carrying capacity is defined as the level of tourist activity or tourism which creates impacts on the host economy and environment that are acceptable to the hosts, yet allows the tourists to enjoy themselves in a way that is sustainable for the future. Thus the number of tourists, their length of stay, the degree of seasonality (time concentration), the spatial concentration of the visitors and the actual characteristics of the tourists and the destination are all important in defining this optimum level.

Figure **5.1** shows that as the volume of visitors increases, so does their impact. Other negative features develop which may influence the socio-cultural impact. It therefore follows that a threshold limit can be established beyond which the impact becomes unacceptable or intolerable. This is known as the **saturation limit**. This is often reached very easily where tourism intensity is augmented by day-visitor recreational activity, as for example in accessible national parks such as the Peak District.

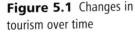

Figure 5.1 Changes in tourism over time

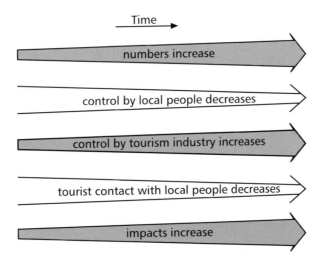

There is no one absolute measure for determining the carrying capacity of a particular area. However, comparing similar areas may be helpful in arriving at a reliable threshold limit. It must also be remembered that host acceptance of the tourist presence may change over time. It is common for the socio-cultural carrying capacity to increase as the hosts become more used to tourists and accept them (see **Chapter 6**). However, it can decrease dramatically after a series of unfortunate experiences with tourists (see **6.6** on page 65). There are four major aspects to carrying capacity which are shown in **5.2**. Usually the carrying capacity threshold is initially exceeded at a destination in one aspect.

Figure 5.2 Aspects of carrying capacity

Physical

This relates to the amount of suitable land available for facilities. It also includes the finite capacity of facilities (such as car-parking spaces, tables in restaurants, or bed spaces in accommodation). It is the most straightforward of all capacity measures, and can be used for planning and management control (by, say, limiting car-parking spaces at sensitive sites). It is sometimes called **through-put capacity** – i.e. the maximum number of people that can be coped with per booking period.

Psychological/perceptual

The psychological (or perceptual) capacity of a site is exceeded when a visitor's experience is significantly impaired. Of course, some people are 'crowd tolerant' and enjoy busy places, while others shun them. Psychological capacity is therefore a very individual concept and difficult to influence by management and planning. Landscaping can be used to reduce the impression of crowding. Forests have a high perceptual capacity.

Biological/environmental/ecological

The biological capacity of a site is exceeded when environmental damage or disturbance is unacceptable. This can relate to both flora and fauna, although more work has examined the capacity thresholds of vegetation (for example, at picnic sites, along paths, or in dune ecosystems) than has looked at the tolerance of animals or birds to tourism. It is also important to consider the total ecosystem (such as the Norfolk Broads) rather than individual elements.

Social/cultural

The concept of a social carrying capacity is derived from ideas of community-based tourism planning and sustainability. It attempts to define levels of development which are acceptable to the host community residents and businesses. The social structure of a small community and the rarity or uniqueness of the local culture are key factors.

The reality is that the concept of carrying capacity is easy to understand, but very difficult to assess. The difficulty is not helped by the diversity of factors that have a bearing on it (**5.3**).

EXTERNAL

■ **Tourist characteristics**

The development of mass tourism will cause carrying capacity to be exceeded much faster than explorer or adventurer types.

■ **Type of tourist activity**

This will determine the nature of the tourists. The provision of casinos can offend local cultural life-styles and will cause community leaders to claim that the threshold is reached because of fears of gambling, vice, etc.

■ **Opinions of the tourists**

The volume and nature of the tourist presence on beaches, facilities, etc. will influence tourist satisfaction rates and future carrying capacity.

■ **Planning, management and technology**

The quality of planning and management will affect the appropriateness and effectiveness of any strategy designed to keep developments within the carrying capacity.

INTERNAL

■ **Social structure**

For example, a tribal longhouse in Sarawak will have a much lower carrying capacity than a multi-cultural urban area.

■ **Culture**

Unusual or unique cultures will have a lower carrying capacity and will be very vulnerable to commercialisation.

■ **Environment**

Natural environments are far less resilient to tourism than are built environments (except for archaeological or historic sites). Delicate, fragile environments include tundra ecosystems and coral reefs.

■ **Economic structure**

The more developed the economy, the less vulnerable it is to mass tourism. Over-rapid expansion in LEDCs leads to excessive leakage from the economy.

■ **Resources and infrastructure**

These can have a very direct bearing; their main impact is one of limiting capacity, e.g. local water supplies or the ability of the local airport to handle large aircraft.

Figure 5.3 Checklist of factors influencing carrying capacity

Review

3 Define the term **carrying capacity** as used in studies of tourism. What is the justification for distinguishing between physical, biological, psychological and socio-cultural capacities?

4 Why is it difficult to assess the tourist carrying capacity of an area?

5 Choose your own examples to illustrate each of the factors in **5.3**.

SECTION C

The environmental impacts

There is a fundamental relationship between the environment (from wholly natural to built) and tourism. It is the original environment that attracts the tourists in the first place, whether it be scenery or historic heritage. In theory, the relationship should be mutually beneficial. The tourists enjoy beautiful environments. Using revenue generated by tourists, these environments are protected to maintain their quality for both posterity and current tourism activity.

So much depends on the nature of the tourists themselves and the style of tourism. As tourist flows increase, tourism can become a major generator of environmental problems. This is well borne out by the Galapagos case study (**Chapter 8 Section C**). Unless successful management strategies are evolved, the costs can soon outweigh the benefits. This is especially true where there is over-use of relatively small areas of land or ocean that are both fragile and vulnerable to damage. Pressures on coasts, mountains, national parks, historic monuments and historic city centres are some of the most serious.

Factors that influence the equation between environmental costs and benefits include the following.

- **The nature of the tourism** Clearly, mass tourism has the potential for both a more intense and more widespread impact, but sometimes quite low-volume tourism can have a disproportionate effect. This is exemplified by the damaging effects of trekking in the Himalayas. Until recently, there has been a singular lack of management along the 'Kleenex trail' in Nepal, where litter and waste disposal are major problems.
- **The nature of the destination** This is linked to the degree of spatial concentration of tourism. The built environment in urban areas is relatively durable to high-volume visits. Organisational structures can plan for large flows so that environmental damage rarely occurs. Other places, such as small-scale historic sites like Stonehenge, the Acropolis in Athens or the Lascaux Caves in France (which had to be closed and replaced by a replica experience) are especially vulnerable to damage. Most grassland ecosystems are vulnerable to trampling (**5.4**). For this reason, visitor flow management is a key feature of sand dune and sloping grassland sites.

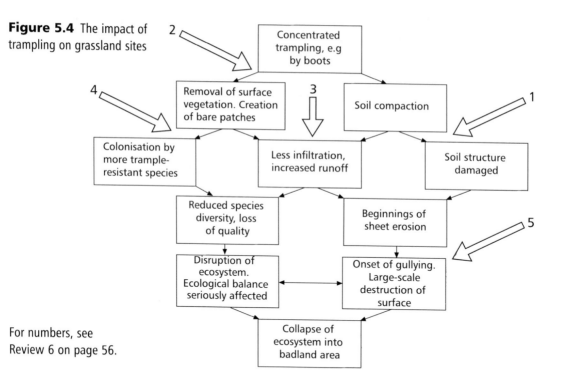

Figure 5.4 The impact of trampling on grassland sites

Concentrated trampling, e.g by boots

Removal of surface vegetation. Creation of bare patches

Soil compaction

Colonisation by more trample-resistant species

Less infiltration, increased runoff

Soil structure damaged

Reduced species diversity, loss of quality

Beginnings of sheet erosion

Disruption of ecosystem. Ecological balance seriously affected

Onset of gullying. Large-scale destruction of surface

Collapse of ecosystem into badland area

For numbers, see Review 6 on page 56.

- **Types of activity** Some activities such as motor-cycle scrambling, mountain biking and skiing are claimed to be more inherently damaging than others.
- **The time dimension** In theory, it is beneficial if tourism is seasonally concentrated. This means that there is a recovery period every year, for example for tracks and possibly from pollution effects. However, within the tourism season, activity tends to be more concentrated. Much depends on whether it is the growing season or the wet season. Constant year-round activity in wet weather conditions is the most damaging of all.

Many of the damaging aspects of tourism on the environment are summarised in **5.5**. However, there are, of course, some benefits, the main one being that tourism supplies the cash to conserve natural areas, to support conservation programmes and conservation of endangered species, to rehabilitate old buildings and sites and provide new facilities. High-quality interpretative features such as the submarine trails for snorkellers can provide experiences of environmental appreciation and education of the highest quality. A balanced approach would emphasise how planning and management can either avoid the worst consequences or attempt to reverse some of the damage to the environment caused by tourism. Examples of this include the following:

- Pollution is a major environmental negative impact, but cleaning programmes are in place to protect the attractiveness of the location to tourists (for example, the famous Copacabana beach in Rio de Janeiro is made pristine every dawn).

Environmental component	Tourist developments and tourist activities	Environmental consequences	Located examples	
Water	Discharge of garbage and sewage into sea, lakes and rivers. Release of oil from recreational boats, cruise ships, ferry boats, etc. Bank erosion.	Contamination and health hazard to local people and tourists; change in and destruction of aquatic plant and animal life. Less aesthetic value. Increased toxicity in water bodies – detrimental to aquatic plants, contaminated seafood. Problems for bathers; problems of water supplies.	Issues around the Mediterranean and along coral reef coasts of Caribbean and Florida.	NATURAL
Atmosphere	Increased travel to tourist destinations, especially by car. Growing significance of recreational driving; tour buses in destination area.	Air and noise pollution, especially in peak seasons – loss of recreational value; adverse impact on plant and animal life.	Problems of air pollution in historic tourist towns, e.g. Chiang Mai (Thailand) and in national parks such as Yosemite (USA).	
Coasts and islands	Sun, sand, coastal developments of resorts, campsites, golf courses and other facilities. Access roads, provision for cars. Airport/heliport development, marinas.	Loss of coastal environments, e.g. mangrove swamps. Destruction of coral reefs. Loss of land for traditional uses. Issues of beach erosion. General loss of attraction.	Developments near Nandi, Fiji. Development along Thai coastline, e.g. Pattaya Beach and Phuket Island. Development of Oahu (Honolulu).	
Mountains (areas of wilderness)	Trekking, mountaineering. Skiing. Construction of hotels, mechanical lifts, power lines, sewerage systems, etc.	Deforestation leading to soil erosion. Increased footpath erosion and litter. Loss of vegetation to create ski pistes. Increased landslides and avalanches. Potential for visual pollution and increased water pollution.	Trekking in Nepal. Ski tourism in Alpine areas (French Alps, North American Rockies).	
Vegetation	Deforestation for resort construction, increased use of fuelwood. Fire dangers in parks and forests. Trampling impacts at honey-pot sites (cars and pedestrians). Collection of flowers, plants and fungi.	Structural alteration of plant communities. Degradation of forests – increased runoff and erosion. Risk of fire in high-value park areas. Constant trampling – disappearance of fragile species. Increased damage of plant habitats.	In Nepal. Along coasts of Borneo. Tourist developments in national parks (Thailand). Kakadu National Park (Queensland, Australia).	
Wildlife	Indiscriminate and planned hunting and fishing. Poaching wildlife for souvenir industry. Chasing and harassing wildlife for photos. Development of trails and highways through natural areas. Speeding vehicles.	Reduction of wildlife numbers, especially of endangered species. Disruption of feeding and breeding, predator–prey relationships. Relocation of feeding and breeding areas. Disruption of wildlife migrations, etc. Drainage of wetlands.	Safari tourism in East Africa. Issues of endangered species such as elephants, rhinos (tusks, horns, etc.). Coto Doñana in Spain.	
Archaeological, historic and religious monuments	Excessive use for recreational and tourist purposes.	Overcrowding – excessive on site: trampling, litter. Alteration of original function, commercialisation. Potential desecration – alteration of original use and function. Vehicular access: air pollution issues.	Pont du Gard, France. Management of Knossos, Crete. Overcrowding issues at Stonehenge, Taj Mahal (India) and the Pyramids. Destruction of the Sphinx by air pollution. Town centres, especially in historic towns	
Town centres, especially in historic towns	Expansion of hotels, restaurants, bars, entertainment facilities, souvenir shops, etc. Increased car and coach traffic, many visitors	Displacement of residents; disruption and overcrowding through traffic congestion; overloaded infrastructure; increased pollution and noise from late-night tourist activities. Unpleasant architecture of new developments.	Problems of Florence and Venice. Management of tourist traffic in Bath, Cambridge, Canterbury, Chester.	BUILT

Figure 5.5 A summary of the environmental impacts of tourism

Review

6 Refer to diagram **5.4** on page 54 and suggest the management strategies you might employ at stages 1–5 (identified by the arrows) in order to arrest the sequence of decline.

7 Write an essay about the impact of tourism on one of the environmental components shown in **5.5**.

8 Are you convinced that there are many environmental benefits to be derived from tourism? Justify your viewpoint.

- Whilst soil erosion and trampling are endemic, tourism revenue can be used to finance ground repairs, as for example using geotextiles at Malham Cove in the Yorkshire Dales National Park.
- Biodiversity is threatened but tourism revenue is used to protect endangered species such as the panda and to establish new conservation areas and projects such as the Annapurna scheme in Nepal.
- Whilst infrastructure may be challenged by tourist over-use, the tourist use can also conserve it. For example, tourist patronage has helped to save vulnerable branch railway lines such as the Heart of Wales line. Tourism can also lead to the building of new roads, the survival of village shops and services, and provide much-needed water and electricity supplies for local people (as in northern Chile).
- Although tourism and the controversial 'right to roam' can encroach on farmland, it can also provide the revenue (via farm tourism) to actually keep marginal land in production.
- Tourism buildings are frequently visual eyesores, but a tourism complex built on derelict land can enhance a site, as at Festival Park, Stoke-on-Trent (pages 45–46).
- Tourism revenues can be recycled to plan and manage tourism more effectively. Revenue may be derived from pricing policies, exclusion controls, wilderness permits and vehicle admission controls, all of which require the collection of fees. Possible expenditures include developing new sites with interpretative trails to disperse tourist activity and take pressure off honey-pot sites (as in Dartmoor National Park) and providing wardens to educate the public at such sites.

In the final case study of the Galapagos (**Chapter 8 Section C**), you will have the opportunity to consider these issues, as tourist taxes of around US$5 million are generated there each year. They could be used solely for national park management, but currently are not.

Enquiry

1 Look at the four case studies in **5.6**. Using the information provided and, where possible, your own supplementary research, assess the degree to which the environmental costs of tourism outweigh the benefits in each case.

2 Study **5.7** on pages 58–59, which is a checklist of what to look for when assessing environmental damage. Visit a local natural or built environment site and carry out an audit of possible damage. Devise a fieldwork programme which would enable you to investigate damage on the site.

A The world's coral reefs

About 60 per cent of the world's coral reefs are at risk. Some 1 million species are believed to live on coral reefs, including more than 25 per cent of all the species of marine fish. Although there are more than 400 marine parks and reserves around the world, most are very small and 40 coral-reef countries lack any protected areas.

Over 100 countries benefit from tourism related to coral reefs, from the Cayman Islands in the Caribbean to Israel and Egypt with their Red Sea coasts.

The worst affected coral-reef areas are in South-East Asia where over 80 per cent of reefs are under threat from coastal developments and fishing. Other problems include cyanide and dynamite fishing, pollution from the shore and ships, and damage caused by tourist snorkellers standing on the reefs.

B Vanishing archaeological treasures

Every year more tourists visit the legendary home of the Minotaur at Knossos in Crete. As many as 5000 people visit on a peak day. The Minoan palaces are made of very soft stone which is being worn away by sheer tourist pressure. The mosaic floors are a major problem. A £300 000 project, largely funded from tourism revenues, aims to build new walkways and reinforce roofs, at the same time closing some areas to the public.

In the Valley of the Kings (Egypt) Tutankhamun's tomb faces complete collapse. Archaeological excavations and effluent from a now demolished tourist lavatory are the causes. There is a great fear that flash floods, channelled by gullies eroded by hoards of tourists, could cause irreparable harm, especially to the priceless wall paintings in the tombs.

C Trekking and wrecking in Nepal

After foreign aid, tourism is Nepal's main source of income. Every year around a quarter of all tourists (300 000) visit national parks and conservation areas such as Annapurna. They leave litter (known as the 'Kleenex trail'); by burning fuelwood to heat water and cook, they encourage forest destruction; and the yaks which carry their supplies overgraze mountain pastures.

Park fees from tourism raise only a fifth of the running costs. The trekking routes are lined with non-biodegradable litter, scattered in piles on the outskirts of villages or on river banks. In the absence of toilet facilities, pollution of the water supplies has become a major problem. Along the trekking route seven large tourist lodges have been built within forest clearings. Rare species such as the Red Panda are threatened.

D Ski damage in the Alps

Over the past two decades, the tourist industry in the Alps has boomed. Stunning scenery and excellent skiing attract tourists all year round, often bringing economic salvation to remote valleys. Huge areas of forest have been destroyed to make way for ski pistes, cable cars, holiday buildings and roads, exacerbating landslides and avalanches. Vegetation was bulldozed aside, including arctic tundra vegetation above the snowline which is irreplaceable.

Every time an area wins the right to stage the Winter Olympics, enormous environmental destruction occurs as extensive facilities are established. Downhill skiing is considered to be the most damaging of the Alpine activities.

Figure 5.6 Four contrasting case studies of the environmental impact of tourism

Figure 5.7 Checklist of the environmental impacts of tourism – an environmental audit

	Strongly evident	Evident	No evidence	Not an issue
THE NATURAL ENVIRONMENT				
A Changes in floral and faunal species composition				
1 Disruption of breeding habits.				
2 Killing of animals through hunting.				
3 Killing of animals in order to supply goods for the souvenir trade.				
4 Inward and outward migration of animals.				
5 Destruction of vegetation through the gathering of wood or plants.				
6 Change in extent and/or nature of vegetation cover through clearance or planting to accommodate tourism facilities.				
7 Creation of a wildlife reserve/sanctuary.				
B Pollution				
1 Water pollution through discharges of sewage, and spillage of oil/petrol.				
2 Air pollution from vehicle emissions.				
3 Noise pollution from tourist transportation and activities.				
C Erosion				
1 Compaction of soils, causing increased surface runoff and erosion.				
2 Change in risk of occurrence of landslips/slides.				
3 Change in risk of avalanche occurrence.				
4 Damage to geological features, e.g. tors, caves.				
5 Damage to river banks.				
D Natural resources				
1 Depletion of ground and surface water supplies.				
2 Depletion of fossil fuels to generate energy for tourist activity.				
3 Change in risk of occurrence of fire.				
E Visual impact				
1 Facilities, e.g. buildings, chairlifts, car parks.				
2 Litter.				

	Strongly evident	Evident	No evidence	Not an issue
THE BUILT ENVIRONMENT				
A Urban environment				
1 Land taken out of primary production.				
2 Change of hydrological patterns.				
B Visual impact				
1 Growth of the built-up area.				
2 New architectural styles.				
3 People and belongings.				
C Infrastructure				
1 Overload of infrastructure (roads, railways, car parking, electricity grid, communications systems, waste disposal, water supply).				
2 Provision of new infrastructure.				
3 Environmental management to adapt areas for tourist use, e.g. sea walls, land reclamation.				
D Urban form				
1 Changes in residential, retail or industrial land uses (move from houses to hotels/boarding houses).				
2 Change to the urban fabric, e.g. roads, pavements.				
3 Emergence of contrasts between urban areas developed for the tourist population and those for the host population.				
E Restoration				
1 Re-use of disused buildings.				
2 Restoration and preservation of historic buildings and sites.				
3 Restoration of derelict buildings as second homes.				
F Competition				
Possible decline of tourist attractions or regions because of the opening of other attractions or a change in tourist habits or preferences.				

CHAPTER 6

The human impacts of tourism

The economic impacts

Tourism is seen by most nations as a way of helping to expand the economy. The generation of international tourism enables a country to earn foreign currency. It thereby helps to achieve a positive balance of payments account. Tourism is always referred to as an **invisible export**. Worldwide tourist trade was valued at $350 billion in 1996. It is a small wonder therefore that nearly all countries think that they should share in this wealth.

The **travel account** is the balance of receipts from tourism compared with the estimated expenditure by the country's citizens as tourists abroad. Countries such as Spain, France, Italy, Turkey and Greece show a surplus, while countries such as Japan, Germany and the UK show a deficit, largely because they generate such large numbers of tourists. However, in balance of payment terms, the apparent deficits are turned into surpluses because these countries control multinational companies, airlines and banking, all of which feed back capital.

Many LEDCs have the potential to make money from tourism in that they have the resources to host tourism. However, as yet their citizens do not have the wealth to be international tourists. Although it is possible to list many economic benefits of promoting tourism, in reality the balance between economic benefits and costs is not as favourable as it might seem. For example, the profit margin is reduced by the leakage of profits to foreign developers and by having to import special goods for the tourists (**6.1**).

Figure 6.1 How leakage occurs

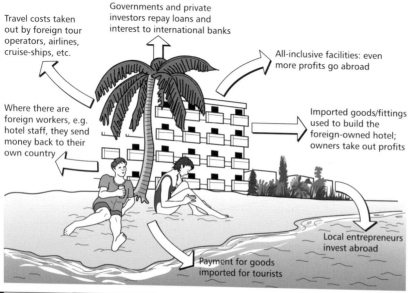

Travel costs taken out by foreign tour operators, airlines, cruise-ships, etc.

Governments and private investors repay loans and interest to international banks

All-inclusive facilities: even more profits go abroad

Where there are foreign workers, e.g. hotel staff, they send money back to their own country

Imported goods/fittings used to build the foreign-owned hotel; owners take out profits

Local entrepreneurs invest abroad

Payment for goods imported for tourists

Tourism and development

Tourism aids economic development in a number of ways. Clearly, foreign exchange earnings are of vital importance. These can be enhanced by levying such things as tourist and airport taxes. For LEDCs, hotel and resort construction have such high capital costs that they can only be undertaken if there is **inward investment**. The trend in tourism, as in other service industries, is towards greater **globalisation** of operations. Hence large multinational companies are increasingly involved, often operating as conglomerates with shares in airlines, hotels and even travel agencies. The World Bank also provides help in financing some capital projects. Tourism thus promotes development through the encouragement of new economic linkages with the outside world.

Tourism is the world's largest employer. It also creates an enormous range of jobs both directly and indirectly. Tourism's labour demand is pyramidal in structure. At the top, there is a small core labour force of full-time, highly-paid and multi-skilled managers. They are supported by a very large number of workers, often poorly paid, who are engaged in low-cost, labour-intensive functions, such as cleaning. Often the better jobs in tourism do not go to local people, but there are plenty of opportunities for local entrepreneurs to make a living.

By encouraging diversification, tourism can play a part in supporting marginal rural economies. For example, it can provide additional support for hill farms or dairy farms hit by EU milk quotas (**Chapter 4 SectionC**). There are also many instances of urban tourism helping the regeneration of central- and inner-city areas (**Chapter 4 Section D**).

Multiplier effects

Figure 6.2 The multiplier effects of tourist spending

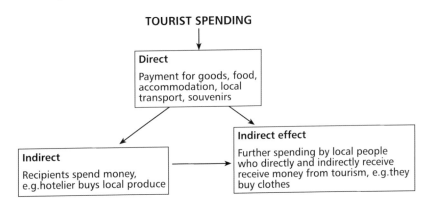

Finally, we need to note that tourism generates its own multiplier effects (**6.2**). Essentially, as a resort develops so does the local economy. As profits from tourism increase and become more widespread, so profits begin to **trickle down** into the local economy. In an ideal situation, this should lead to the emergence of more local suppliers and a decreasing reliance on foreign imports. The multiplier effect can also improve the quality of local services by creating money for investment and by encouraging a more buoyant demand. The multiplier effect can also be demonstrated at a national level (**6.3**).

Figure 6.3 Measures relating to tourism in selected island economies (1990)

Country	Income multiplier	Tourism receipts (US$m)	GNP (US$ m)	Tourist dependence (receipts/GNP)	Tourist density (tourists/capita)
Sri Lanka	1.59	75	90	1.2	0.02
Jamaica	1.27	407	7 936	19.5	0.35
Dominica	1.20	9	90	10.0	0.56
Cyprus	1.14	497	8 747	17.6	2.22
Bermuda	1.09	357	12 388	34.7	7.11
Fiji	1.07	169	1 893	14.2	0.37
Seychelles	1.03	40	1 096	27.4	1.55
Malta	1.00	149	1 864	12.5	2.46
Mauritius	0.96	89	668	7.5	0.27
Antigua	0.88	114	6 669	58.5	2.59
Hong Kong	0.87	2 211	13 266	6.0	7.02
Philippines	0.82	647	1 359	2.1	0.02
Bahamas	0.78	870	45 327	52.1	6.17
W Samoa	0.66	7	45	6.4	0.29

The strength of the multiplier effect and the magnitude of its economic impact varies according to a range of factors. These include:

- The **level of development** of the local economy – in other words, what it can supply for the expansion of tourism.
- The **type of tourist** – in theory, elite tourists should spend more.
- The **organisation of tourism**. A contentious issue is how much all-inclusive and cruise-ship tourism actually put back into the local economy.
- The **ability of the local economy to supply** a range of tourist needs such as attractive souvenirs.
- The **level of leakage** and the possibility of minimising it (**6.1**).

The downside

A case has been made to show the economic benefits of tourism, but there are some concerns which can outweigh the benefits.

- Tourism is a volatile industry on which to base economic growth (see **Chapter 3 Section D**).
- Tourism in LEDCs can increase dependence on foreign companies which leads to extensive leakage (**6.1**). For example, in Vanuatu in the South Pacific (a 'hot' destination for the year 2000), 90 per cent of the profits go to foreign companies.
- Tourism can be so effective in regenerating an area that it can lead to localised inflation. This in turn can have a major impact on local people when it comes to buying food and using services.

- Questions are frequently raised about tourism's ability to generate a career structure of employment for local people, even where they have appropriate skills and qualifications. In areas such as the Philippines, a mass rural exodus to work in hotels has led to labour shortages in intensive rice farming.
- Negative externalities result for example from the over-use of water and the consequent fall in the water table. The overloading of sewerage systems and huge traffic congestion can also cause problems for the local economy.

Case study: Victoria Falls, a town dedicated to tourism

In 1998 Zimbabwe hosted more than a million tourists, nearly all of whom visited Victoria Falls, a World Heritage site. In the words of a local travel agent, 'Victoria Falls have something for everyone'. Tourism flourishes in the Falls area and nearby game parks. The industry provides plenty of job opportunities for the working population of the town, which has now grown to over 20 000 residents (**6.4**). Tourists are unaffected and unaware of the strikes and riots in the capital Harare and other major cities. Everyone claims to enjoy their visit to Victoria Falls as there is so much to do.

Figure 6.4 The multiplier effect at Victoria Falls

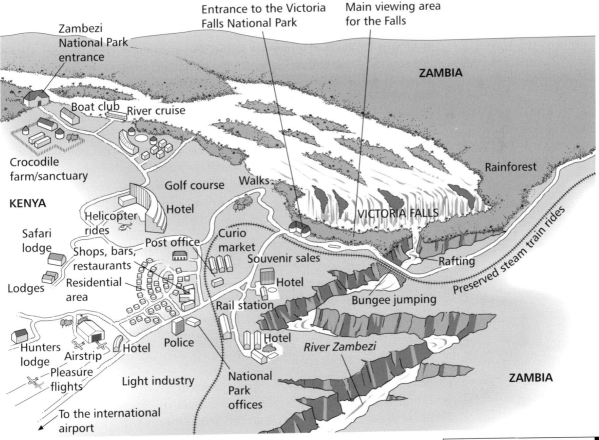

The town of Victoria Falls was built for tourism and could be regarded as the archetypal tourist trap. The 'kitsch' curio shops, traditional tribal dance shows, reptile parks, adrenaline adventure sports, marimba 'muzak', the buzz of low-flying helicopters over the Falls and the zebra-striped tour buses are all part of the town's tourist jungle.

Fortunately the star attraction, the Victoria Falls themselves, are safely cornered off and protected as a national park.

Review

1 Look at **6.1** which illustrates the concept of leakage. Explain the main ways leakage can occur. How would you minimise its impact?

2 Explain why the distinction is made between **direct** and **indirect** multiplier effects.

3 Draw up a table summarising the main economic costs and benefits of tourism in a destination country.

4 Do you think that there are any differences between LEDCs and MEDCs in terms of the economic impacts of tourism?

The socio-cultural impacts

Contact with the local people

Clearly the socio-cultural impacts of tourism will depend on the type of tourism as well as the type of tourist. Smith's typology of tourism combines the type of tourist with the volume of tourism (**6.5**). He makes the point that, in general, independent explorer tourists fit in best with the local environment and community. This is because of their relatively small numbers, the slow rates of growth in their type of tourism activity and their potential for community involvement. It is ironic that the recent (January 1999) deaths of tourists in Yemen were of the type of tourist who was genuinely interested in the Yemeni people and their culture. Package tourists usually arrive en masse to facilities that have been built rapidly, often with fewer links to the local economy. They meet local people in shops and bars or as workers in their hotel ('my friend the barman', etc.) or possibly as hawkers on the beach (where a feverish sales pitch can annoy the tourists). Genuine exchanges of ideas or lengthy conversations are more likely to occur with independent travel.

Figure 6.5 Smith's typology of tourism

Type of tourist	Number of tourists	Adaptations to local norms	
Explorer	Very limited	Accepts fully	
Elite	Rarely seen	Adapts fully	
Off-beat	Uncommon but seen	Adapts well	Socio-cultural conflict
Unusual	Occasional	Adapts somewhat	
Incipient mass	Steady flow	Seeks Western amenities	
Mass	Continuous flow	Expects Western amenities	
Charter	Massive arrivals	Demands Western amenities	

It is generally argued that the greater the divergence in terms of culture and living standards between the tourist and the host, the more likely relationships are to be unsatisfactory. Doxey's index of irritation illustrates this correlation (**6.6**). The flow diagram links the relationships to time, suggesting that unless careful management strategies are developed, host irritation will increase dramatically.

Figure 6.6 Doxey's index of irritation

Levels of host irritation

Time

 EUPHORIA
Initial phase of development: visitors and investors welcome, little planning or control.

Visitors taken for granted. Contexts between residents and outsiders more formal (commercial). Planning concerned mostly with marketing.
 **APATHY**

 **ANNOYANCE**
Saturation point approached. Residents have misgivings about tourist industry. Policy-makers attempt solutions by increasing infrastructure rather than limiting growth.

Irritations openly expressed. Visitors seen as cause of all problems. Planning now remedial, but promotion increased to offset deteriorating reputation of destination.
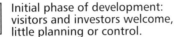 **ANTAGONISM**

Figure 6.7 Symbiotic tourism on Atata

Spatial proximity is another key factor. Enclave tourism behind barbed wire, as in the planned resorts of North Zanzibar, is deliberately sanitised so that local people will not ruin the tourist beaches. Where tourism is dispersed throughout a community, as is the case with trekking in Nepal, relationships can be more effectively cultivated. Tourism based on small hideaway islands with local communities can create particularly sensitive situations. An example of good practice in such situations is provided by the small island of Atata, some 30 minutes by boat from the capital of Tonga in the South Pacific (**6.7**).

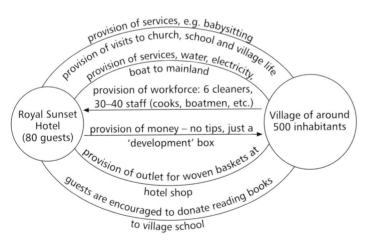

Royal Sunset Hotel

'One of our attractions is a nearby "working" Tongan village, which guests can visit.'

All guests must:
- follow a dress code when entering the village
- only go to the village on formal visits (tours)
- offer no alcohol to staff.

Case study: The Maldives – give us your money and space

In the Maldives Islands in the Indian Ocean, tourists are welcome for their dollars but are almost always kept in isolation on atoll islands that have been specifically developed as resorts. There are now nearly 80 such island developments, with more planned. Release of the islands for development is strictly controlled by the Government.

Tourist numbers have grown rapidly and are expected to reach 300 000 by the year 2000. Apart from the island on which Male International Airport is located, visitors are barred from the many inhabited islands unless they have a permit to visit a local family or are on an organised small-boat cruise or helicopter visit. In this situation, local people queue up to sell to the tourists, of whom they see so little. Except for these organised trips and hotel staff, tourists meet no local people. Careful security at the airport prevents the import of drugs, alcohol and pornographic literature. As is made clear in the literature provided for tourists, the Maldives are wholly Islamic; the 220 000 inhabitants must not be tainted. There is a strict behaviour code once you arrive at the resort. No nude and topless bathing (women) is permitted. If caught, both the tourist and their hotel have to pay a hefty fine.

The main tourist activities are water-based. Here are some of the best coral reefs in the world. Relaxation is high on the agenda for all the tourists.

The Maldives government argues that separation has happened by coincidence rather than design. It goes on to say, however, that the smallness of the islands (they average 400 metres across) makes separation necessary if tourists want beaches to themselves rather than sharing with local people. From the tourists' point of view, it probably does work because for a short time they can imagine themselves cast away on a sort of paradise desert island, albeit an air-conditioned one.

Marketing culture

There are many elements of culture that attract tourists. They include handicrafts, traditions, history and architecture, local food, as well as art and music, religion and traditional dress and ways of life. There are major concerns about the manner in which indigenous cultures are used to promote and sustain international tourism. There is also the related issue of authenticity. Local people are required to present their culture in a way to please and attract tourists. The development of dance and music in Bali as a result of tourist revenue and interest is always cited as a positive cultural outcome, but in many cases, such as the 15-minute visits of safari buses to Masai villages in Kenya, the dances are very staged. Equally staged are the Hawaiian feasts where pseudo-folk nights for package-deal tourists are produced to order. Such nights can be excuses for heavy drinking, over-eating and poor tourist behaviour.

There is major concern that craft industries from native tribes are being taken over by Far Eastern traders. Their poor-quality, non-authentic work and cheap prices mean that genuine quality indigenous craft work is not able to compete – hence the setting up of fair trade organisations like Traidcraft.

People behaving badly

A second area of concern focuses on the way the nature of tourist–host contacts can alter the value systems and moral basis of traditional society. A seemingly casual life-style combined with conspicuous consumption and the flouting of dress codes can have a very bad impact. A growing number of young males are attracted to the life-style of tourists (known as the **demonstration effect**). Many argue that the damage caused to so many young males goes beyond blue jeans and electronic gadgets to hooliganism and increased gambling, prostitution and crime. This is often linked to the organisational structure of casinos and entertainment areas. Tourism may not cause the crime, but it can provide an environment for cultural degeneration. There are inevitably conflicts between tourism and religious customs, with many Muslims and Hindus concerned about the devaluing of mosques and temples by large numbers of 'culture gazers'.

An overview

In summary, the socio-cultural impact equation must take account of a range of possible costs and benefits.

- Debasement and commercialisation of cultures.
- Revitalisation of handicrafts, many with the traditions long forgotten.
- Revival of performing arts and rituals.
- Introduction of new and more modern values and practices which encourage entrepreneurism.
- Travel is one of the great forces for peace and understanding.
- Risk of promoting activities such as gambling, alcoholism and prostitution.
- Empowerment of women in new jobs in tourism, sometimes in sex tourism.
- Rising crime amongst local people.
- Commodification of traditional practices and customs into tourist-friendly performances.
- Issues involved in the demonstration effect.
- Tourism can help people sell their culture in a favourable light.
- Erosion of local languages; introduction of English (American) language and culture.
- New patterns of local consumption often using imported goods.
- Promotion of the hosts' cultural reputation in the global community.
- Increased tension often between 'elders' and youth and between imported and traditional life-styles.

As with all these impacts, management is the key to success. An example of good practice is provided by St Lucia in the Caribbean where children are being taught the importance and economics of tourism and how to foster good relationships with visitors. All this augurs well for the future of tourism on that lovely island.

Case study: The socio-cultural impact of tourism in the Khumbu region of Nepal

Nepal is one of the poorest countries of the world. Every year it is visited by over 300 000 tourists, 30 per cent of whom go on a trekking holiday. There are over 100 tour companies offering holidays, including the Everest trek. Whilst the environmental damage is well documented by articles on the 'Kleenex trail', the socio-cultural impacts of trekking on village life are of equal concern. The Khumbu valley is a highland region in Nepal (6.8). It is the main source of the Sherpas who carry the packs and guide trekking expeditions. Traditionally, the people in Khumbu were subsistence farmers, growing staples such as potatoes and vegetables and rearing livestock (including yaks) on high pastures by means of transhumance. Surplus products were traded with Tibet. Fuelwood was the main source of energy.

The trekking industry has brought many changes to the region.

- The break-up of traditional village life: young men have severed links with their villages.
- Many families now have second homes in Kathmandu. They leave the Khumbu region for part of the year so that they can run their businesses; 21 companies are Sherpa owned. Some men have a wife in Kathmandu as well as in Khumbu.
- There is often not enough labour in the region to do the agricultural work; this is now done largely by women.
- There are many more double-storey houses now. Poor landless men can earn enough as porters to rebuild their houses. Even glass can be flown in via Lukla.
- Fuelwood is getting scarce and expensive (the trekkers use it for cooking).
- All building materials are now brought in from lower down the valley.
- Land and house prices have gone up, especially in the main village of Namche Bazaar which is now totally dependent on tourism.
- Trekkers stay in commercial lodges, some of which have been set up by local businessmen. There is now an oversupply of beds, especially since the building of a new Japanese hotel in the area.
- Yak breeding is no longer a central part of the economy, although there is a huge demand for yaks as pack animals.
- Villages look more prosperous. Many young men working in businesses in Kathmandu send back money to their parents and wives.
- Electricity is now supplied by a mini-hydro scheme financed by trekking revenue.

- Although traditional potatoes are still important, Sherpas buy rice and eat Western food when trekking. Diet is now more varied and consequently health standards have improved.
- Traditional garments are no longer made. Western-style clothes and ex-expedition kit are common.
- Sir Edmund Hillary (the first man on Everest) helped to build and equip schools in the region, so education has improved.
- Many students drop out of education to take apparently high-earning jobs in tourism.
- Many Sherpas suffer injuries and even death from carrying huge packs for tourists' expeditions. Sherpas are poorly trained in health and safety and are not assured of compensation when injured.
- Families are breaking up: men living away from home means that women are left to cope.
- Women are deprived of the security and companionship of husbands, except in the monsoon season when trekking stops.
- Demographically there is a surplus of young unmarried women in the villages. Population is declining in the villages as deaths outnumber births.

Figure 6.8 Khumbu trekking flows and facilities

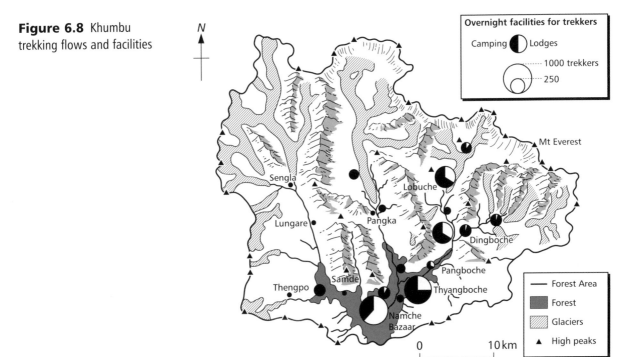

Review

5 Study **6.7** and explain why the management of the Royal Sunset Hotel is considered an example of good practice in tourism.

6 Identify the good and the bad points of the visitor strategy adopted in the Maldives.

7 Classify the points made in connection with the socio-cultural impact equation (page 67) as either **costs** or **benefits**. Is the overall balance positive or negative?

8 Write a structured evaluation of the economic and socio-cultural impacts of tourism on the Khumbu valley, Nepal.

SECTION C

The human rights issue

To visit or not to visit? This is a question conscientious tourists must ask themselves when considering a possible holiday in a country where human rights abuses are known to have taken place. China, for example, may be the world's fastest-growing tourist destination, but should so many people be supporting a country where political freedom is in such short supply?

You could argue that by going to countries with poor human rights records you can expose their oppressive regimes. This might be done by drawing attention to the plight of the oppressed, but it is unlikely, however, given that most tourist experiences are highly sanitised. In many cases, local guides are hand-picked and specially trained to toe the political line and convey the right sorts of message to foreign visitors. The chances are you will have a wonderful time, meet charming hotel staff and see beautiful sites. The reality is that your dollars could finance an oppressive government and add political legitimacy to them.

Sometimes human rights abuses are taking place in countries as a direct result of tourism. The current situation in Burma (renamed Myanmar) is an extreme example. The Burmese military regime declared 1996 'Visit Myanmar Year' with the aim of attracting 50 000 tourists to shore-up a contracting economy. To prepare for the arrival of the hoped-for tourist, many hundreds of poor people were forcibly relocated to make way for tourist developments or to clean up the areas around top religious sites. At the same time, thousands of people, including women, children and the sick, have been forced to work on construction projects such as roads and other aspects of tourism infrastructure. They live in labour camps in atrocious conditions, with many workers dying of exhaustion, malnutrition and disease. All this just to welcome tourists and to convey a false image.

Many travel companies offer Burma in their brochures as an exotic opportunity. In the words of one tourist: 'When we booked nobody mentioned the terrible regime. After learning about the situation we decided we couldn't go. You couldn't enjoy a trip knowing your hotel was built by child labour, could you?'

Other tourism-related human rights abuses include:

- Tourism industries that thrive on sexual exploitation of women and children, as in India, Cambodia, Thailand and Sri Lanka. Children are sold by poor families for as little as £50 or kidnapped for the 'skin trade'.
- Displacement of native people, such as the Samburi pastoralists of northern Kenya, by the creation of nature reserves for wildlife tourism. In this specific instance, the people have been relocated in arid lands. They are denied access to the only waterhole in the area, which is now a swimming and game-viewing area for tourists staying at a luxury hotel. Equally, the protection of species in reserves means that predators kill livestock outside the park.
- Local people are frequently forced from their lands and fishing areas by tourist developers who require the sites for luxury resorts and golf courses. Often pitiful levels of compensation are paid. This is a problem in many Far East and South-East Asian locations which rely on a Japanese trade that demands super-luxury facilities.

Review

9 Do you think tourists should consider human rights issues before they book a holiday?

10 Can you justify the view of some tourists that it is better to go and see the issue for yourself?

Enquiry

1 Tourism is a very important component of many island economies. Study **6.3** on page 62 and answer the following questions:
   a Why are some of the countries more dependent on tourism than others?
   b In which countries do the statistics suggest there has been less leakage?
   c What are the implications of the varying levels of tourist density for the islands concerned?
   d To what extent can you see correlations between the levels of economic development (as measured by GNP) and tourism receipts? Give reasons for the relationship you have identified.

2 Study **6.4** on page 63.
   a Assess the statement that Victoria Falls have 'something for everyone'.
   b Make a photocopy of **6.4** and shade in all the direct employment opportunities available in tourism.
   c Assess how the factors shown in **6.2** have influenced the magnitude of the economic impact of tourism at Victoria Falls. You should use any guidebooks on Zimbabwe, or the Internet, to supplement the information in the case study.

Can tourism become sustainable?

The new tourist

Many writers on tourism suggest that as the tourist market in MEDCs matures, a new kind of tourist will emerge with some of the following essential characteristics.

- **Experienced** and therefore wishing to move on from the short-haul package beach holiday to more innovative travel such as adventure-, activity- or ecotourism. A cruise would be appropriate for those wanting more tame, cosseted adventures.
- **Sophisticated**, as a result of previous and frequent travel experiences, for example in a 'gap' year pre- or post-university as a 'round-the-world tourist'. The new tourist is able to cope with multi-cultural and demanding overseas environments.
- **Educated** to require rewarding activities to fill their leisure time and satisfy cultural, intellectual and sporting interests.
- **Knowledgeable** through experience and exposure to the media about a range of destinations.
- **Demanding** in that experience makes for a more critical comparison of the suppliers and products before choosing and during the holiday, as a result of greater awareness of consumer rights. A diet of 'Watchdog', *Which* and passenger charters with supporting legislation have led to a complaints culture. Inevitably large companies with their broad appeal suffer more poor publicity than smaller niche operators.
- A well-developed **social conscience** with a concern for culture and the environment.
- **Stressed** by the rat race and by demanding employment. This characteristic will require a different response from the travel trade than all the previous ones.

It is claimed that the arrival of the new tourist will tend to favour a more bespoke form of tourism. Modern technology will allow every tourist to be treated as an individual customer. The prediction is that specialist niche operators will flourish, while larger operators will use technology to customise a product to individual tastes. This feature is already apparent in the long-haul market and in some current brochures.

As in other industries, competition in a crowded marketplace is forcing operators to seek maximum efficiency. Every year, a significant number of operators go bankrupt as intense competition drives prices down. Information technology is seen as a major facilitator, because it is able to provide a database of customers and their needs. It can be used to manage facilities more effectively to deliver maximum throughput and to target marketing via junk mail and telesales. At a macro level, linkages between providers will be encouraged, leading to integrated reservations systems that will become a superb marketing tool. Linkages can result in Global Distribution Systems (GDS) which market all at the same time a wide range of products such as hotels, rent-a-car and ground transportation for independent travellers. The Internet is already having a major impact on the tourism industry, perhaps at the expense of travel agents, as it encourages sophisticated choice by the new tourists who often purchase holidays and flights direct.

As with other industries, the need for efficiency has led to the formation of large companies. Many of them operate **transnationally** to secure maximum **economies of scale** in marketing and the use of technology. They are also good for protection in an industry which is subject to rapid change and uncertainty. Large companies can spread risks and can cope with the seasonality of tourist flows by worldwide deployment of aircraft. This has tended to lead to **globalisation** of the industry. It is interesting to note that most large travel companies contain within them around a dozen smaller 'niche' companies. In spite of this, **commodification** of holidays is still very apparent, especially in Britain. Concerns are expressed about these multinational companies in that they can assume a neo-colonial relationship and lack sensitivity to the host country's needs.

Figure 7.1 The expanding pleasure periphery, from a European perspective

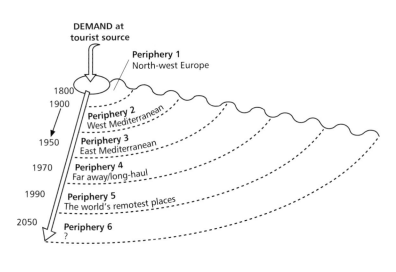

Figure **7.1** shows the concept of pleasure periphery. This depicts the boundaries of tourism surging outwards like a giant tidal wave across the Earth as tourists constantly seek new experiences. There is no doubt that tourist statistics support this concept.

As tourism has now become the world's largest single industry, it is increasingly seen as an employment opportunity. The new tourist demands a high quality of human resource as part of the high-quality product, with frequent recourse to complaints if it is not supplied. Suppliers need to develop training programmes to generate the level of service demanded. The training of personnel will inevitably increase costs in what is a labour-intensive industry. Lower staffing levels can harm the pampered luxury feel of travel. The new tourist is increasingly concerned with value for money, which does not necessarily mean a cheap product – more a fair reflection of the quality provided. Many last-minute bookings for cut-price holidays lack the necessary quality assurance and generate a disproportionate number of complaints.

The tourist industry will need to adopt sophisticated planning and management techniques in order to provide a high-quality and rich experience for the tourist who is increasingly aware of the need to protect the environment. Hopefully such people will begin to influence the industry by insisting on green choices.

As the Secretary-General of the World Tourist Organisation wrote in 1995: 'Travel and tourism will inevitably continue to increase. Meeting the growth in a responsible, sustainable way, that preserves and enhances the beauty and attractiveness of the destinations, is a challenge.' It is the hope of many environmentalists that the mass tourism of the 20th century will be replaced by green tourism in the 21st century.

Review

1 Think about your friends. Do you see in them any of the characteristics of the new tourist? How many of them are happily booking mass tourism holidays to Greece, Spain or Turkey?

2 a Make a copy of **7.1** and then add some examples of particular places described in earlier chapters.

b Devise a pleasure periphery model from a North American perspective.

3 Can you make any suggestions for places in periphery 6 in the 21st century – or do you think the 'edge' has been reached?

Ecotourism – myth or reality?

The damaging effects of some forms of intensive tourism on the environment and the people of an area are well documented in **Chapters 5 and 6**. Whilst there are many examples of successful and imaginative tourism that bring genuine economic benefits to a community without significant damage, the norm presents a depressing picture. More worrying is the fact that it is growing even more common as the tourist industry grows.

All sorts of solutions have been put forward to develop alternative tourism. The current buzz-word is ecotourism, which is the fastest-growing sector, albeit from a low base. In 1998 it was estimated that 5 per cent of the total market claimed to offer 'ecotours'. **Ecotourism** is described as 'an economic process by which rare and beautiful ecosystems and cultural attractions are marketed internationally to attract tourists'. Therein lies the inherent contradiction, so clearly seen in the case studies that follow. It is not sustainable tourism as such. Once the flow of tourists increases, the potential damage and destruction becomes harder to manage and it escalates, as for example in Costa Rica and even Dominica (see page 76). Many would argue that ecotourism can only be truly sustainable when it is small-scale, as in the Zanzibar study (pages 9–11) or in the Ecuador rainforests example (pages 78–79). The extended enquiry based on the Galapagos Islands (**Chapter 8 Section C**), now at a cross-roads in its development, looks at a number of directions tourism there might take. The one area where the nations of the world have to get it right is in the pristine environment of Antarctica (**Section C**). This area can be viewed as a test case where a number of approaches to planning and management have been adopted that may make the tourism sustainable – that is, 'conserving the environment for future generations'.

The guiding principles of **sustainable tourism** are:

- The environment has an intrinsic value which far outweighs its value as a tourism asset.
- Long-term survival must not be prejudiced by short-term considerations.
- Tourism should be recognised as a positive activity with the potential to benefit the destination and its community.
- A prime aim should be that the local community participates in the industry and its development.
- The relationship between tourism and the environment must be managed, with the ultimate sanction of the withdrawal of tourism to ensure the environment is conserved.
- Tourist activities and developments should respect the scale, nature and character of the place they are sited in.
- In any location, harmony must be sought between the needs of the visitors, the place and the host community.

In effect, sustainable tourism requires an up-grading of environmental and socio-cultural interests and a down-grading of purely economic aims. At its best, ecotourism is notable for the way it approaches the planning and management of tourism environments.

- It aims to build responsible tourism by developing tourism with dignity, and managing capacity.
- It encourages conservation by the education of both local people (the St Lucia School project) and the tourists (via the Green Tourism movement). It leads by example with both the quantity of sites conserved and the quality of their management.
- It develops an environment focus by solving environmental problems and exporting ecotourist ideas around the world, such as the imaginative experiment in village tourism in Zimbabwe known as the Campfire Project.

Case studies: Belize, Dominica and Costa Rica

Belize

Belize, the former colony of British Honduras, started to promote tourism in 1983 as a means of earning foreign exchange and to further economic development. In 1985, 100 000 tourists visited; by 1997 this had risen to 300 000. Belize has always promoted ecotourism with the designation of protected areas and with maximum community involvement. However, the sheer volume of visitors means that Belize ecotourism is increasingly 'old tourism in new clothes'. This is exemplified by the much-publicised US$50 million development at Ambergris Cay. According to one travel writer, this development now offers 'pleasant upmarket holidays in a beautiful place for the American market'.

Dominica

This Caribbean island is closely associated with ecotourism. In spite of an initial desire to go for mass tourism similar to the rest of the Caribbean (usually the '3S', or 'sea, sand and sun' variety), a report in 1975 suggested that the way ahead was in the selected development of small-scale, nature-based tourism. A national park (Morne Trois Pitons), a national historic park (Cabrits) and national forest reserves were established. Accommodation is dominated by small 'mom and pop' family-run hotels and guest houses, 75 per cent of which are owned by Dominicans. By 1995 tourism contributed 5 per cent of GNP.

There is some concern for the future: a target of 80 000 stay-over tourists for the year 2000 (compared with 30 000 in 1991) may be excessive. There are also plans:

- to construct a large cruise-liner pier near the National Historic Park (cruise tourism tends to be both space- and time-intensive)
- to expand the Melville Hall Airport to accommodate jet aircraft
- to build a 100-unit American-style hotel.

All three proposed actions are indicative of a desire to increase the volume of tourism. Other concerns, even at present levels, include the problem of inadequately trained guides, and poorly maintained trails that are vulnerable to erosion in the heavy rainfall. The over-concentration of tourists in accessible sites is beginning to produce all the features of 'honey-pot' damage.

Dominica is facing the perennial ecotourism dilemma: how to attain an appropriate balance between development, and the biological carrying capacity (the most easily exceeded of all aspects of carrying capacity).

Costa Rica

Costa Rica is at present regarded as one of the most advanced ecotourism destinations in the world. It has much to offer tourism. It is politically stable, shows features of a middle-income country (what Americans would describe as 'civilised'), and yet it has exceptional biodiversity with 12 discrete life zones with distinct flora and fauna. It is also bounded by two contrasting ocean coasts. A comprehensive scheme of both public and private conservation areas means that 20 per cent of the country is protected (**7.2**).

In the 1980s Costa Rica developed a marketing strategy for a range of nature and adventure trips (ecotourism) but also encouraged '3S', cruise and business tourism. The ecotourism sector is a rapidly growing market. The Costa Rica Expedition Agency (CREA) alone – just one of 30 companies in the market – now attracts 20 000 clients annually. The CREA delivers its tourists to a large number of village- or community-based conservation areas, such as La Selva Biological Field Station. The $300 000 it earned from 13 000 ecotourists is a vital source of revenue for the villagers, most of whom are involved in the running of the Station.

National parks such as Volcan Poas (accessible from San Juan) are victims of their own success. Over half the 500 000 tourists who visit Costa Rica each year (a million expected by 2005) visit a national park during their stay. To combat visitor overload, and also to generate more money for management, an increased visitor fee structure has been discussed but not yet implemented. The widespread nature of the conservation areas and their large size mean that there is an opportunity to disperse visitors, but this has not yet been achieved. There is no national plan to push for this. Excessive use of the accessible areas is causing water pollution by campsites, overcrowding, trail erosion and changes in wildlife behaviour. Whilst there are management plans, these are rare and the Park Service is suffering from a lack of trained wardens and research personnel. It needs to create more revenue.

A broader issue is what is happening to the 80 per cent of land outside the conserved area. This is suffering from huge agricultural pressures and widespread habitat loss, especially of rainforest. There are some excellent examples of ecotourism projects, often in the smaller private reserves, but Costa Rica's environmental image will surely become tarnished if ecotourism continues to expand and the parks are increasingly stressed by the sheer volume of visitors.

Many travel companies and countries have been quick to pick up on the public enthusiasm for exotic environments. They are keen to market small-group tours to faraway places as ecologically-sound tourism, or ecotourism. These tours are designed to ensure that travellers get a worthwhile, almost unique, experience. Inevitably they are expensive, often based in luxury lodges and using small-group transport. Environmentalists dismiss many of these tours as **ego-tourism**, and claim that it is ordinary tourism dressed up in a politically correct form and given a green veneer. Whilst some ecotours do fulfil the

Figure 7.2 Protected areas in Costa Rica (1992)

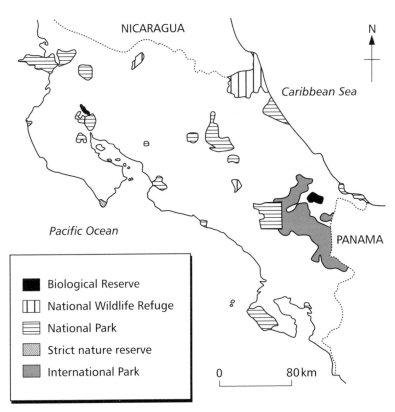

NICARAGUA

Caribbean Sea

N

Pacific Ocean

PANAMA

Biological Reserve
National Wildlife Refuge
National Park
Strict nature reserve
International Park

0   80 km

requirements of sustainable tourism, they remain quite rare. If ecotourism is to work, it has to fulfil two conditions:

- it must limit the number of visitors to a level that the environment can sustain
- it must be set up and run in co-operation and consultation with local inhabitants.

The process too has to be right. It should take the form of a genuine environmental and educational experience. Many people would argue that only small-scale tourism can meet these conditions.

Case study: Small-scale ecotourism in eastern Ecuador

The Napo region is located in the rainforest zone of Eastern Ecuador. The indigenous population of Quichua Indians got the idea of developing ecotourism in 1990 after a group of tourists came to stay with a local family who were paid for the privilege.

Figure 7.3 The Quichua regulations for ecotourism

The Quichua people insist that all visitors must abide by certain rules and regulations.

Exchanges of clothing or other personal items with community members are not allowed. Nor are community members allowed to accept gifts.

When walking in the rainforest:
• do not touch any branches without looking carefully first. They may carry thorns, dangerous insects or even snakes
• do not pull on branches on vines – they may fall down on top of you.

Visitors should never go off for a walk alone. It's easy to get lost in the rainforest.

Do not enter people's houses without being invited in.
Do not make promises you may not be able to keep (e.g. to send back photos after the visit).

All rubbish, e.g. empty bottles and tubes, must be taken away by the visitors.

If you need to go to the toilet, and facilities are not immediately available, go to the side of the rainforest track, never in or near a stream or lake.

Avoid any displays of affection, even with close friends. In this community it is considered rude to hold hands or kiss in public.

Always check first before touching plants or animals. They may cause a rash, or sting you. Do not collect any plants, insects or animals unless you have permission to do so.

In 1991, ActionAid (a British charity) carried out a research project which recorded how the rainforest in the Napo region was being destroyed by a combination of oil exploitation and rainforest tourism, thus threatening the Quichua's traditional life-style. An ecotourism project was developed in an attempt to strengthen the community in order to create a sustainable income for the indigenous people (**7.3**). Visitors come from the USA and Canada and are usually committed environmentalists. They travel into the area by canoe, and then a two-hour hike through the forest. Stays last for up to six days and include walks through the 'jungle', visits to community projects such as the garden of medicinal plants, and to see traditional pottery-making. Tourists in groups of up to 12 overall stay in buildings built by the local people.

The Quichua use their expert knowledge of the forest as the basis for the guided tours. They have trained their children, via an ecological training programme in the village school, to recognise the plants and their uses. Money from tourism has led to major improvements of services in the villages.

In 1996, the Ecuador Government banned the Quichua from running tours in the Napo region, because it feared the local project was not benefiting the national economy. The Government claimed that the Quichua were not registered as tour guides and did not pay any taxes on their earnings. The Government has since threatened to arrest local community leaders if they continue to run tours. Converting this informal scheme to an official one and developing a booking and management structure for such a remote area is a key issue. In spite of its excellent intention and its achievements, the scheme may well be abandoned.

Whilst ecotourism is one of the fastest-growing sectors, developed largely by smaller dedicated tour companies, its spectacular growth is from a very small base and it still constitutes less than 5 per cent of the market. It is not a concept that blends well with the large globalised multinational companies which the modern economics of tourism have promoted. Many of the large companies, for example the Inter Continental Hotel Group, are making overt attempts to become more environmental in terms of their management of waste, water and energy, with extensive recycling schemes. Other companies, such as British Airways, have carried out a green audit of their business practices, and spend substantial sums on rewarding green tourist initiatives. The cynics would claim that these strategies are good politics and generate a good public relations image.

The way ahead

Tourism is an ever-expanding industry with a voracious appetite for resources, especially new land for development. This is often at the expense of interests of local people, as in Goa or Zanzibar, where they have little chance of recovering an equitable share of the profits from tourism that 'leak' abroad. It is also apparent that there may be some little time before the 'new tourist' profile permeates throughout the potential market.

For the next 20 years, transport to an exotic paradise, requiring little or no organisation or planning, with the express desire for relaxation, will be a strong market segment. It is an approach endorsed by the mass tourism operators. Two new strands of development, namely **cruise-liner tourism** and **all-inclusive resorts**, are also developing very rapidly. The tourism companies find that these are selling very well, and they can be operated for maximum profit. Whether they come any closer to being sustainable is very much open to question.

Review

4 Define the terms **ecotourism** and **sustainable tourism**.

5 In your own words, explain each of the guiding principles of sustainable tourism (page 75).

6 Read the three case studies of Caribbean environmental tourism again (pages 75–77). Do you think any of these three countries is providing genuine ecotourism? Justify your viewpoint.

7 What do you see as the obstacles to the promotion of ecotourism?

8 Refer to the case study on the Napo region of Ecuador (pages 78–79).
  a Outline the development of the scheme.
  b Identify the features of the scheme that make it a genuine ecotourism project.
  c Analyse the problems that threaten the future of the scheme.

Antarctica – making ecotourism work

You have probably come to the conclusion that ecotourism can work very effectively on a small scale. But can the sustainability that is such an essential component be effectively developed and managed in a large-scale area such as Antarctica? This is the world's last great wilderness. Because of the pristine quality of Antarctica's natural environment, ecotourism has simply got to be made to work.

The ultimate destination

'Until you have been there for yourself you cannot imagine this desert of ice. No words can really describe the sheer magnitude, the awe, the wonder and the excitement you will feel on your first zodiac trip. This is the last frontier of tourism – it is an adventure of a lifetime to visit the planet's crystal wonderland.'

An ecstatic tourist

Antarctica is an unusual destination in that it is not populated, except by scientists at a small number of permanent research establishments. Polar scientists have always been very concerned about tourism because they fear it would interfere with their scientific work and destroy the near-perfect environment. On the other hand, committed tourists can be very supportive of such scientific work by publicising it and helping to raise funds.

In the 1980s, Antarctica represented the very edge of the pleasure periphery (**7.1**). Only just over 30 years earlier, in 1956, the first plane flew in with tourists, and two years later the first ship brought tourists to Antarctica. Today tourism is a thriving business with (in 1998) around 10 000 tourists visiting, 95 per cent of them in cruise-ships.

The nature of tourism

Essentially Antarctic tourism is of three types:

■ Very expensive camping trips for naturalists, photographers and journalists.
■ Ship-board visits largely by cruise-ships but also by converted Russian ice-breakers. Most start either in Ushaia, the nearest port, or in Port Stanley (the Falkland Islands) (**7.4**).
■ Over-flights – These have restarted after an interval of nearly 20 years following the crash of an Air New Zealand DC10 on Mount Erebus, which killed all 250 passengers.

Tourists come for the scenery, glacial landscapes and wildlife viewing (especially seals, whales and penguins) as well as for the remoteness and isolation and the chance to test themselves in adverse weather conditions. Tourism is therefore concentrated in the short southern summer period from mid-November to March. Tourists are also interested in historic sites, as for example McMurdo Sound with its huts dating from the Scott and Shackleton expeditions.

Figure 7.4 Antarctica and the southern continents

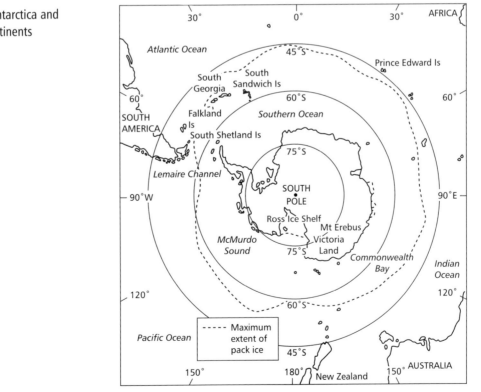

Ship-borne tourism in Antarctica follows the **Lindblad pattern**, named after an early pioneer of this type of tourism. Cruises are termed 'expeditions', and the expeditionary concept is reinforced by the issue of polar-style clothing. As most of the ships are comparatively small, with average capacity of between 50 and 100 people, the ship-based programme of educational lectures from Antarctic specialists leads to a cohesive and motivated group. Tourists are carefully briefed on the requirements of the Antarctic Treaty and the Environmental Protocol. They are informed of the code of conduct in terms of behaviour when ashore, adherence to health and safety requirements and rules regarding wildlife observation. When visiting any one of around 200 possible sites (tourists are free to land anywhere except at designated special preservation areas or near active scientific research areas), the overall group (maximum size of around 100) is divided into zodiac boatloads of around 20, each led by an expert guide. Sites may only be visited every two or three days. Strict rules are laid down for all 'expeditions'. Guidance is described as 'thorough and positive'. All the major tour operators are members of the International Association of Antarctic Tour Operators (IAATO). IAATO is in effect a self-regulating body.

The environmental impact

Current Antarctic tourism has been described as being, in almost all cases, of a high standard. So far as the environment is concerned, tourist behaviour and impact have tended to be regarded as benign. Until recently, the main issue was the lack of detailed research on the impacts of tourism. That situation is now being rectified by research undertaken mainly by the Scott Polar Research Institute in Cambridge. It has investigated some high-pressure sites like King George Island and Elephant Island in the South Shetlands (**7.4**) as well as all 200 approved landing places. Their findings, published in 1997, were as follows:

- Antarctic tourism is a well–run industry, living up to its sound record for environmental concern.
- Most (not all) tour operators are members of IAATO and do a good job in terms of promoting sound practice.
- Guidelines are widely accepted by operators and tourists alike but they need to be updated to include the Environmental Protocol.
- Damage to vegetation (especially the fragile moss mat) is due to natural causes such as breeding seals. Tourists are usually scrupulous in not walking on fragile vegetation areas. Further research on compaction by boot trampling is needed.
- No litter is attributed to tourists; tourists are very concerned about waste seen around the scientific research stations.
- Virtually no stress is caused to penguins by tourists visiting their breeding colonies. However, tern colonies seemed to suffer from disturbance.

- Seals are largely indifferent to the human presence. Tourists who follow wildlife guidelines cause no impact. Infringements are few, but there is a need to keep miscreant photographers under control.
- Out of 200 landing sites surveyed only 5 per cent showed any wear and tear. These need to be rested, but at present there is no mechanism to implement this sort of management.

The future

There are plans for the number of tourists visiting Antarctica to rise threefold – perhaps to reach 30 000 by the year 2020. This will clearly mean more ships. In 1996 there were 120 cruise-ship visits. More visits and more tourists inevitably increase the potential for pollution incidents in the dangerous waters.

At present tours are high quality and highly priced (around £7000 per head). The season is also very short and limited by natural constraints. Many operators would like to maintain their high profit margins. They see some obvious ways of doing this.

Using larger ships carrying up to 500 passengers is one way. However, for safety, shore parties of over 100 are not feasible unless some sort of high-density, national-park style sites are developed. Arctic wildlife refuges in Alaska have shown that they can cope with such numbers, so perhaps they may be developed in the Southern Hemisphere too. Clearly only one visit ashore can be undertaken each day, so entertainment such as games and videos may need to be provided. For Antarctica, small-ship tours have proved very successful. Larger ship size means less cohesion and less unity of environmental commitment.

Another possible way is to cut costs on quality of field staff. This will mean reducing numbers of staff, and employing people trained to a lower level, or less renowned academically. Again this is likely to lower standards.

An expanded system would be increasingly difficult to police, and self-regulation may collapse unless inspection systems are developed. There is the added problem of a growth in flight-seeing and flight-tourism. Increased over-flying by light planes and helicopters is a real problem for penguins and other birds during the breeding season.

Review

9 Well, what do you think?
  a Is Antarctic tourism genuine ecotourism?
  b Is it sustainable as currently practised?

No land tourism from hotels is currently planned, and permission would be refused. A major base with hotel and pier at Vesifold Hills was considered, but only briefly before it was thrown out. At present there are no overall management schemes for tourism in Antarctica, although many have been discussed and drafted. The creation of ASTIs (Areas of Special Touristic Importance), as currently operated in South Georgia (7.4), would prevent encroachment on protected areas that are usually only informally marked. The setting up of interpretative museums of polar scientific work and history would certainly help to 'educate' the tourist. Realistic tourism management strategies need to be developed to cope with a future scenario of less ethical tour companies and less responsible tourists.

Looking to the 21st century

SECTION A

A 2020 vision

It is estimated that global tourism will, on average, grow by 4 per cent per annum over the next two decades or so. This will mean a threefold increase between 1998 and the year 2020. As part of that rise, other trends may be expected.

- Not only will a bigger proportion of the total population travel for leisure, but they will be drawn increasingly from LEDCs. Continued development in those countries will allow people to acquire the time and money to travel.

- In the MEDCs more people will go on holiday more times a year – perhaps as much as four or five times a year.

  - Business tourism (30 per cent of the market) is expected by some to increase exponentially. Others would disagree and argue instead that video-conferencing will actually inhibit this kind of tourism.

  - People will journey further and extend the **pleasure periphery** (**7.1**). By 2020, one in three trips will be long-haul compared with one in four in 1998.

  - Tourism will become more diversified. There is already a huge range of niche operators who are capable of meeting the needs of specialist markets. The Internet will reinforce this trend. Already birdwatchers, train buffs, wine tasters, politics fanatics and choral singers are very well catered for – who next?

  - Tourism will become more widespread. The relentless quest for new unspoilt paradises will continue.

Clearly the 2020 vision requires us to expect more growth and yet more growth. An unregulated tourism industry can only lead to further environmental and social degradation, as well as new problems such as transmission of diseases. The industry is controlled by big, often multinational companies, which are concerned primarily with economic success. Surely, there must be an instinct of enlightened self-preservation that will force them to rethink their development strategies of unregulated and poorly managed growth (**8.1**). Will the industry regulate itself and how?

Figure 8.1 The future shock of ever growing tourism

Review

1 Study **8.1**. What is the basic message of this cartoon?

2 What would you suggest might be done in order to make the industry better organised in the 21st century?

SECTION B

The role and responsibilities of government

It is an inescapable fact that governments have a huge and ever increasing responsibility to influence, perhaps control, the development of tourism. So *planning* is the key word. Planning is vital in tourism for the following reasons:

- To shape and control physical patterns of development at national, regional and local scales.
- To ensure that the tourism sector develops in an integrated way with other economic sectors.
- To provide a long-term framework for future development.
- To organise a strategy for marketing and promotion.
- To conserve resources, some of which will become increasingly scarce, for example water and biodiversity.
- To plan for the sustainable management of the tourism industry.

Unplanned tourism, with unregulated, haphazard development, is both inefficient and costly. Economic, social, cultural and environmental costs will almost certainly outweigh the benefits. As tourism is such a rapidly changing industry there is a need for continuous planning. The desired sequence of events is shown in **8.2**, whilst **8.3** summarises some of the areas of responsibility covered by tourism planning.

Tourism planning at a national level will look at tourism development as:

- a foreign revenue earner
- a provider of jobs
- a vehicle of regional and local regeneration
- a means of supporting a national interest in environment and heritage regeneration
- a means of improving and extending physical infrastructure
- a medium for creating an awareness of the country on the international stage.

Through tourism planning, governments have the ability or potential power to influence or even control:

- the rate of tourism growth
- the type of tourism
- the location of developments
- the relative roles of the public and private sectors or multinational enterprises versus community-based tourism.

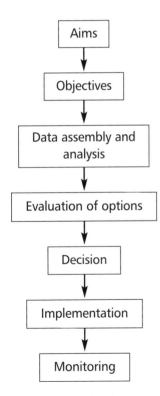

Figure 8.2 The planning sequence

They tend initially to have economic goals (improving the trade balance, creating employment, etc.) and see tourism as creating a **spread effect** outwards from designated tourist enclaves. Increasingly, however, the reasons for government involvement in tourism are related to social and environmental goals. Often economic goals are dramatically in conflict with other overall development aims. Maximum income generation is usually linked to high-volume tourism. As we saw in **Chapter 5**, this type of tourism has the greatest potential to damage the environment. Strong local participation increases the likelihood of developing alternative and more environmentally-sensitive tourism. While alternative modes may also be expected to reduce leakages, they are likely to involve a lower expenditure by a smaller volume of tourists. In short, they will be lower money-earners.

Physical	Economic	Socio-cultural	Environmental	Business
■ Land development controls ■ Zoning ■ Location and design of activities ■ Transport ■ Utilities	■ Sectoral investment ■ Creation of jobs ■ Job training schemes ■ Distribution of government grants ■ Production of statistics ■ Infrastructure investment	■ Degree of integration of tourists and hosts ■ Hospitality ■ Authenticity of tourist experiences ■ Presentation of heritage, culture and language ■ Protection of local customs	■ Pollution control ■ Designation of conservation areas ■ Protection of endangered species ■ Protection and designation of heritage sites ■ Environmental health risk assessment	■ Advertising ■ Promotion campaigns ■ Business plans ■ Sponsorship deals ■ Product control ■ Tourism information

Figure 8.3 Areas of responsibility of tourism planning

National governments can influence tourism development in a number of ways.

- By playing a major role in providing infrastructure in the form of roads, airports and services to open up an area.
- By providing support sources for training of key personnel for hotel administration, tourist office management, or in tourism marketing and research.
- By providing a range of incentives such as grants or subsidies for various types of tourist development such as new hotels, or for new urban attractions.
- By developing planning controls, for example on the quality and type of hotel.
- By legislating on the issue of visas to control the flow of tourists and, in former times in some communist countries, to refuse entry to potential subversives. Also by regulating exchange rates or providing a tourist premium exchange rate to encourage spending.

- By controlling the amount of direct revenue from tourism via levels of tourist tax and entry fees. Most governments have a range of security taxes, airport taxes and 'bed' taxes.
- By controlling the issue of work permits to foreign workers recruited to the industry.

Indirectly, a government influences the quality and style of tours via a range of government establishments, such as tourist boards, and via agencies such as national parks.

Case study: Four contrasting national strategies

Bhutan

Special features:

- a small land-locked Himalayan kingdom
- population 1.6 million, of whom 5 per cent are urban
- one of the poorest countries in the world
- tourist attractions include spectacular mountain scenery and features of Buddhist cultural heritage.

Tourism began in 1974 when the King realised that new hotels built for his coronation could be used for tourism. Tourism in turn would generate foreign exchange and help the socio-economic development of the country.

For many potential tourists, Bhutan represents a sort of Shangri-La – the last survivor of a glorious antique world, only recently opened to outsiders after 300 years of isolation. Initially, the number of foreign visits was restricted to a quota of 2500 a year; that limit is shortly to be doubled. All tourists must be part of an escorted tour to specified locations. They are required to pay a surcharge that currently stands at £60 per day. Trekking, cultural visits and wildlife-watching are the only forms of tourism allowed. All tours must be organised by known, vetted companies. All developments, such as hotels, must use traditional architectural designs. The emphasis is on conservation of the environment and culture by a limited, controlled and monitored tourism.

Bhutan's attitude to tourism is ambivalent. On the one hand the country is keen to reap the economic benefits, while on the other it perceives the industry as 'a serpent in paradise'. Hence the development of a strategy that reflects a tight control on tourist flows and behaviour.

Bermuda

Special features:

- a subtropical island
- population 64 000
- a middle-income country where tourism provides significant income in a thriving business economy
- has a perceived image as the playground of rich Americans.

In the early 1970s, a number of restrictions on tourism were introduced in Bermuda. These included a moratorium on the building of new hotels to keep the island's carrying capacity to a 10 000 bed limit. Timeshare development was restricted to one sample resort, which was created for risk-assessment purposes. Cruise-ship arrivals were restricted to 12 000 people in the high season, and contracts were drawn up with only high-quality operators.

By the 1980s an attitude pervaded the Bermudan tourist industry that it was unique in its up-market character. For this reason it was perceived to be free from competition and secure in its market niche. However, during the 1990s, visitor numbers and tourist expenditure began to fall. A re-appraisal of the tourist product needed to be made. Bermuda is currently trying to woo back wealthy Americans by enhancing the range of its services and the recreational activities that it provides.

'Value for big money' remains the keynote of Bermudan tourism, as the island remains interested only in the discerning and really big spenders. It is anxious to distance itself from the mass tourism of the Caribbean islands. At the same time, the islanders need to be reminded of the importance of tourism to their economy.

Cuba

Special features:

- a large Caribbean island
- population 11 million
- a long-standing communist government
- attractions include fine beaches and a rich heritage dating from the Spanish colonial era.

Before the communist revolution of 1959, Cuba was popular with American tourists. At one time tourism was the third most important 'export' after sugar and tobacco (cigars). Following the revolution, international tourism virtually ceased, but domestic and educational tourism (i.e. subsidised holidays for the Cuban workers) flourished.

In the 1980s the Cubans decided that they needed to encourage mass tourism in order to help them overcome a severe economic crisis. Major resources were allocated to state enterprises, such as Intur and Publicitur, to develop and market tourism. Joint ventures involving public and private capital were set up to construct and upgrade hotels, train staff, provide tourist products such as high-quality souvenirs and tours, and to improve the transport infrastructure. All forms of tourism were to be encouraged, from cruise, beach and heritage tourism to conference and business tourism.

Initially the strategy was quite successful, but major problems increasingly confront the country's tourist industry. These include the fact that the nearest and potentially largest market, the USA, is still closed because of the American embargo placed on Cuba. The consequent reliance on long-haul tourists has placed some stress on the national airline which until recently used only aged Russian jets, with a dubious safety reputation. There are also tensions associated with a dual economy and with the affluence gap between visitors and local people. This gap has only been reconciled by allowing no social contact between ordinary Cubans and tourists. 'Leakage' brought about by a growing dependence of the tourist industry on imported goods, and the scale and speed of the developments in tourism, have had a damaging effect.

Malta

Special features:

- a small island state in the middle of the Mediterranean
- population 367 000
- attractions include a mild climate, some good coastal scenery and a rich cultural heritage.

Malta has a long-established tourist industry based on small hotels and self-catering units. Of the three-quarters of a million tourist visitors each year, 70 per cent come from the UK. The clientele is typically working-class and pensioned. In 1989 the Maltese government decided to take steps to shed the 'cheap and cheerful' tourist image and to try to attract the higher-quality tourist. It reasoned that such tourists would have a higher spending capacity, which would create more revenue for the country. It is still early days to assess whether the initiatives that have been taken are yielding the required results.

Review

3 Outline the main aims of tourism planning at a national level.

4 To what extent do you agree with the view that the development of tourism should be left to the private sector?

5 Evaluate the four national strategies described in the case study. Which one impresses you most? Which do you think will be the most successful in terms of achieving its aims? How do you rate the strategies in terms of achieving sustainable tourism?

SECTION C

The Galapagos Islands – a last chance?

This final section takes the form of an extended enquiry. It investigates the Galapagos Islands, one of the few remaining remote unspoiled paradises.

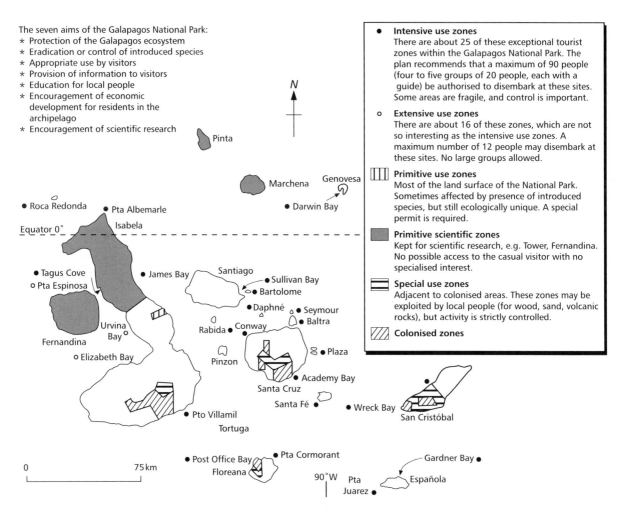

The seven aims of the Galapagos National Park:
* Protection of the Galapagos ecosystem
* Eradication or control of introduced species
* Appropriate use by visitors
* Provision of information to visitors
* Education for local people
* Encouragement of economic development for residents in the archipelago
* Encouragement of scientific research

● **Intensive use zones**
There are about 25 of these exceptional tourist zones within the Galapagos National Park. The plan recommends that a maximum of 90 people (four to five groups of 20 people, each with a guide) be authorised to disembark at these sites. Some areas are fragile, and control is important.

○ **Extensive use zones**
There are about 16 of these zones, which are not so interesting as the intensive use zones. A maximum number of 12 people may disembark at these sites. No large groups allowed.

‖‖‖ **Primitive use zones**
Most of the land surface of the National Park. Sometimes affected by presence of introduced species, but still ecologically unique. A special permit is required.

▨ **Primitive scientific zones**
Kept for scientific research, e.g. Tower, Fernandina. No possible access to the casual visitor with no specialised interest.

▤ **Special use zones**
Adjacent to colonised areas. These zones may be exploited by local people (for wood, sand, volcanic rocks), but activity is strictly controlled.

▨ **Colonised zones**

Figure 8.4 The Galapagos National Park

This destination is at a cross-roads in that it is edging towards unsustainable tourism, having set out some years ago grandiose plans for sustainable ecotourism. In the light of what you have learned from this book, you are left to review the future for this special place.

The story of the development of tourism in the Galapagos Islands (**8.4**), located 1000 km off the Ecuador coast, has been described as 'state ownership with price and quality controls'. There has been a continuous attempt to preserve a priceless natural heritage by a constant policy of limiting access. The issue is not a straightforward case of tourism development versus environmental degradation, as the Galapagos Islands are not at present an area of mass tourism. This is a consequence of their remoteness from the main MEDC markets. The issue includes the problems of a rapidly growing mainland population who are lured by the apparent richness of fish stocks and the prospect of making a living from the international tourism. There are now nearly 25 000 people living on the islands, a huge recent increase. As settlements have grown, so alien species have been introduced such as feral goats which eat turtle eggs, feral dogs which eat lizards, and feral cats which eat birds, lizards and iguanas (**8.5**). These introduced species have also brought with them new diseases that have had a disastrous impact on wildlife and the structure of native ecosystems.

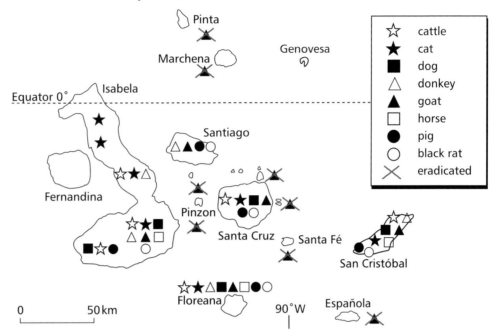

Figure 8.5 Introduced mammals on the Galapagos

A special place

'Formed by volcanic eruptions from a hot spot, the Galapagos Islands lie in isolation off the Ecuador coast. Except for pirates and castaways, the only species to make their way to this mystical, enchanted region were reptiles, birds, plants and fish, who over a long period of time, drifted or flew into its shores. These were the lands which led to Darwin's theory of evolution. Having been untouched for centuries, the creatures from the Galapagos never learnt to fear humans. So rare are some of the species that virtually half of the bird and plant life and all the reptiles are found nowhere else on Earth.'

Quote from a travel guide

What the tourists say

'I will never forget the waved albatross taking off – it needed half a mile to get airborne.'

'I liked swimming with the young sea lions in the surf.'

'Snorkelling over the iguanas feeding was fantastic, but best of all was Tagus cave when we snorkelled with the penguins.'

'Lonesome George [a giant tortoise at the Charles Darwin Research Station] was fabulous – he just kept eating and eating vegetation and watching him lumber off was the highlight of the day.'

The development of tourism

Tourism began on a regular basis in the late 1960s (**8.6**). Tourists almost always arrive by plane at either Baltra or San Cristóbal airport. From

Figure 8.6 Annual flow of visitors to Galapagos National Park (1974–99)

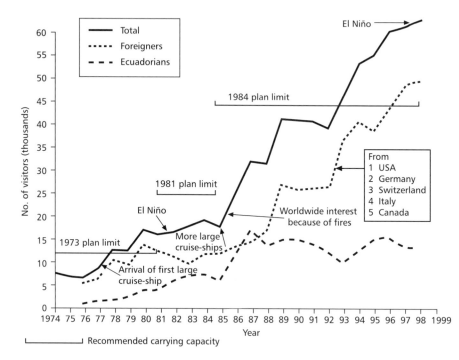

there, they transfer to cruise-ships or take the public bus from Baltra to Puerto Ayora, the centre for day trips and the only concentration of hotels. There are currently about 25 places in which to stay, most of them small (total beds 400–500). Puerto Ayora is something of a boom-town with a huge influx of people from mainland Ecuador who until 1997 had completely free access. The population growth rate is around 8 per cent per annum, with nearly 25 000 people now living permanently on the Galapagos.

Up to 10 planes a day arrive in the high season delivering tourists at the rate of a 1000+ per day. While this flight provision places some restraint on the numbers arriving and leaving, the real control is the capacity of the hotels and cruise vessels. Over 100 boats, including some five large vessels taking up to 100 people each, provide cruises of varying luxury and quality around the islands. The average length of stay is four to five days.

Conservation

In 1959, 90 per cent of the total land area of the Galapagos was designated a national park. As can be seen from **8.4**, only a small part of the total area of the national park is open to tourists. Essentially, the park is zoned and tourists are funnelled towards only intensive use and extensive use zones. The primitive use zones are for independent small-group, backpacker use only, while the special use zones are for scientific study only. The Galapagos management plans have always been big on rhetoric but short on funding. Clear limits and quotas are set for tourist entry. In the late 1970s, the annual limit was 12 000 a year, but by the late 1980s over 50 000 tourists were visiting. Limits were often designated after the quotas had been reached (**8.5**).

By 1997, over 60 000 tourists were visiting with a rising percentage of international tourists (**8.6**). This has boosted the length of stay to six or seven days, thereby putting further pressure on the environment. The tourists come all the year round, so there is not really a high season. In 1986 a marine reserve was designated to include 70 000 km^2 of protected ocean. Japanese intensive fishing was a key problem here and it has proved very difficult to police the area because of its huge scale.

Within the tourist access zones, the Galapagos National Parks Service (GNPS) has introduced well-planned trails and ensured that all groups are accompanied by a guide with some basic training. Since 1996 guide-training has been carefully monitored by the Charles Darwin Research Station (CDRS). There are around 60 possible landing sites, with one or two more identified for future use. The general emphasis of the tours is on education and enjoyment of the environment and wildlife. Every tourist pays a US $100 tourist and park tax and receives a code of conduct. Guides endeavour to ensure good behaviour on all shore excursions and are charged with a range of essential duties to ensure that conservation strategies work.

Management issues

A number of problems of management have been identified.

- Although there is a long coastline, there are few landing sites for the small *pangas* which deliver the tourists from the larger boats. Most of these landings are wet landings, but dry landings made at small piers are more popular with less active tourists. These restricted access points tend to concentrate the human impact; some wear is evident on the trails.
- Although bird breeding rates do fluctuate, they are largely a function of variations in marine productivity. In El Niño years, this productivity is very low as there is no upwelling of the cold current needed to generate plankton. Visitors seem to have little impact on the nesting and chick-rearing of sea birds. Even with careful use of permits to spread boat traffic, some nesting colonies are interrupted almost continuously. So this finding is rather surprising.
- Sea lions (especially the old bulls) have shown increased aggression and nervousness.
- Litter dumped at sea by boats is a major problem. It provides non-natural food for some animals. In some cases, turtles have been known to swallow polythene bags, thinking they were jellyfish, and to have been strangled as a result.
- A few sites have become very congested, as for example the trail up the volcano on Bartolome.

- Coral damage has been caused by boats dragging their anchors.
- The rising tourist tax does not deter the international tourist. In theory, it should be supplying more management money, but somehow the revenue is not reaching either the GNPS or the CDRS.

All these problems will be exacerbated by the rising numbers. There is no certainty that these have peaked. Although they undoubtedly enjoy the wildlife spectacle, not all of the 60 000 tourists are committed environmentalists. The larger the mass of tourists, the more difficult it becomes to police behaviour in protected areas.

Clearly the Galapagos is steadily drifting away from ecotourism and towards mass tourism. Trends in activity levels are set to become unsustainable in the near future. This is in spite of there being an excellent master plan. So will the Galapagos Islands become yet another victim of tourism's failure to keep its growth within carrying capacity limits? Is this last chance to get things right being frittered away? It is sad that recreation and tourism have this tendency to self-destruct, largely through paying so little regard to their resource base. It is ironic that whilst recreation and tourism bring happiness to the lives of millions of people, they have this dreadful capacity to cause misery and disaster in the natural world. Will we never learn?

Extended Enquiry

Read through **Section C** carefully, paying particular attention to **8.4**, **8.5** and **8.6**.

1 Explain why the Galapagos Islands are at a cross-roads.

2 Write a paragraph summarising the essential decisions that need to be made about the Galapagos Islands.

3 Assess the strengths and weaknesses of each of the following development options.

A Control new immigrants to prevent unofficial, unlicensed tourism in hotels and boats.

B Extend the quota in the intensive use zones to 120 visitors, and use them up to three times a day (two-hour viewing sessions).

C Develop more extensive use zones for small-boat tourism.

D Build large hotels with luxury facilities at Santa Cruz, Tortuga Bay and in Puerto Ayora to be fed by a fast vessel which comes overnight from the mainland. These would be for general tourists who want a pleasant couple of days on a boat-trip just viewing the wildlife.

E Develop more tourist boat ventures, including large luxury cruise-liners which could stop at around six designated dry landing sites on three-day tours. The main pier would be at Puerto Ayora.

F Promote areas outside the park to include setting up a number of adventure activities.

G Develop a greater range of educational programmes from the CDRS, especially for the local schoolchildren on the wildlife, and provide further basic training for all workers in the tourism sector to increase standards of service.

H Raise the tourist tax for foreigners and ensure that the extra revenue is paid direct to the GNPS (at present 70 per cent goes to the Ecuador Government).

4 Find out, via the Internet or by looking through magazines such as *BBC Wildlife*, who are the main tour operators. Are they predominantly small specialist ecotour companies or are they large long-haul operators?

5 Review the case study of Antarctica (**Chapter 7 Section C**) and the information on the Galapagos Islands. Compare the two areas in terms of the nature and management of their tourism.

6 'The present style of tourism in the Galapagos is unsustainable. The only way to maintain ecotourism is to develop selected sites for mass tourism.' Discuss.

Further reading and resources

Books

E. Cater (ed.), *Eco-tourism: A Sustainable Option*, Wiley, 1995.

J. Chaffey, *Managing Wilderness Regions*, Hodder, 1996.

C. Cooper, *Tourism Principles and Practice*, Longman, 1993.

J. Croall, *Preserve or Destroy?*, Calouste Gulbenkian Foundation, 1995.

L. France (ed.), *Sustainable Tourism*, Earthscan, 1997.

C. Law, *Urban Tourism*, Mansell, 1996.

E. Laws, *Tourism Destination Management*, Routledge, 1995.

M. Manuel, *Tourism: Our Future World*, CUP, 1998.

M. Mowforth, *Tourism and Sustainability*, Routledge, 1998.

P. Murphy, *Tourism: A Community Approach*, Routledge, 1993.

D. Pearce, *Tourist Development*, Longman, 1996.

D. Roe *et al.*, 'Take Only Photographs, Leave Only Footprints', IIED Wildlife Development Series No. 10, October, 1997.

S. Williams, *Tourism Geography*, Routledge, 1998.

Magazines

'Sustainable Tourism', *People and the Planet* Vol. 6 No. 4, published by Planet 211, Woburn Walk, London WC1.

'Wish you were here', *New Internationalist* No. 245, July 1993.

Resources

The major resource of low-cost materials for 6th-form use is Tourism Concern. It issues a quarterly bulletin called 'Tourism in Focus', as well as an excellent bibliography and numerous study packs.

Tourism Concern, Stapleton House, 277–281 Holloway Road, London N7 8HN.
Website: http:/www.oneworld.org/tourconcern

In addition, a visit to the Travel and Tourism Fair or Adventure Travel Fair, usually held in London in January or February each year, would yield excellent promotional materials and details of websites for up to 200 tourist organisations and travel companies. Good-quality tourist guides such as *Footprints*, *Rough Guides* and *Lonely Planet* are also excellent sources of detailed information.